NGONDRO COMMENTARY

D1599921

His Holiness Garwang Dudjom Lingpa

NGONDRO COMMENTARY

Instructions for the Concise
Preliminary Practices
of the New Treasure of Dudjom

Compiled from the Teachings of
HIS EMINENCE CHAGDUD TULKU

by Jane Tromge

PADMA PUBLISHING

Published by Padma Publishing
P.O. Box 279
Junction City, CA 96048-0279

Printed in the United States of America
99 98 97 96 95   5 4 3 2 1

Cover by Mark Gatter

Library of Congress Cataloging-in-Publication Data
Tromge, Jane
Ngondro commentary: Instructions for the concise preliminary
practices of the New Treasure of Dudjom /
compiled from the teachings of His Eminence Chagdud Tulku
by Jane Tromge
p. cm.
ISBN 1-881847-06-3 (pbk.)
1. Nyingmapa (Sect)—Rituals. 2. Spiritual life—Nyingmapa (Sect)
I. Chagdud Tulku, 1930–. II. Title

BQ7662.6.T73   1995
294.3′438—dc20
                                                                95-18666
                                                                       CIP

ISBN 1-881847-06-3 Paperback

CONTENTS

PREFACE

It has been my very great privilege to compile these ngondro instructions from a wealth of oral teachings offered by His Eminence Chagdud Tulku Rinpoche. Since coming to the United States in 1979, Rinpoche has given these teachings repeatedly, each time with a wonderful warmth of verbal style and each time highlighting different points. In this commentary, the qualities of his spoken words and some of the rich elaboration he provides have yielded to brevity. The goal has been to make extensive information clear and accessible, offering a convenient reference book for practitioners. This, of course, is not meant as a substitute for a direct oral explanation from Chagdud Rinpoche or some other qualified teacher. Rather, I hope the teachings compiled in this volume will instill confidence in those who undertake the *Dudjom Tersar Ngondro* and support their accomplishment of the full commitment of these preliminary practices.

Even a small book such as this one has required the dedicated effort of many people, beginning with Chagdud Rinpoche himself, who has consistently stressed the importance of completing ngondro as the foundation of Tibetan Vajrayana Buddhist practice. His teachings flow from his own completion of ngondro practices, from extensive knowledge of commentaries on the subject, from carefully retained oral teachings on the *Tersar Ngondro* received from His Holiness Dudjom Jigdral Yeshe Dorje, and from his profound meditative realization.

Rinpoche made numerous corrections and extensive editorial suggestions while reviewing the manuscript of this book. Although its style falls somewhere between his engaging verbal presentation and the strict conventions of a classical commentary as he would write it, I believe that its contents have not drifted too far from his intention to offer these precious teachings to Western students in straightforward English. I feel a heavy burden of responsibility for any mistakes, omissions, or lack of clarity in the text, for which I apologize in advance.

In addition to the profound debt of gratitude I owe to Chagdud Rinpoche for entrusting me with this project and supporting its completion, I wish to thank translators Tsering Everest and Richard Barron; transcriptionists Joan Szoboky and Angie Ponder; and the editing and production team at Padma Publishing: Kimberley Snow, Barry Spacks, Mary Racine, and Laeh Steinberg. I am also deeply appreciative of others who read the manuscript and made suggestions, and of my sangha friends at Rigdzin Ling who carried my share of tasks so I would have time to write.

Anything written as a "ngondro commentary" must present itself most humbly, given the existence—though not yet in English—of the superb ngondro commentaries by His Holiness Dudjom Rinpoche and other Tibetan masters, and the recent availability of the beloved commentary by Patrul Rinpoche, the *Kunzang Lama'i Shelung* (*Words of My Perfect Teacher*), in two English translations. Chagdud Rinpoche himself suggested that another commentary was unnecessary. Still, many who find special pleasure and inspiration in his teachings have often requested a book such as this one. May this brief commentary strengthen understanding and meditative experience and support the accomplishment of ngondro. May it serve as a step toward ultimate compassion and enlightenment.

FOREWORD

His Eminence Chagdud Tulku

All traditions of Tibetan Vajrayana Buddhism have ngon-dro practices, but among these the *Dudjom Tersar Ngondro* of the Nyingma tradition is probably the most concise in terms of recitations and sadhana practice. Hidden in the eighth century by Padmasambhava (Guru Rinpoche), it was intended for these degenerate times when few people have leisure to practice. His Holiness Garwang Dudjom Lingpa (1835–1904) revealed this treasure; his incarnation, His Holiness Dudjom Jigdral Yeshe Dorje (1904–1987), clarified the text and taught it widely.

The history of the successive incarnations of Dudjom Lingpa represents an extraordinary demonstration of spiritual potential. He first appeared on this earth, many centuries ago, as the lord among yogins known as Nüdan Dorje, who prayed with enormous aspiration to benefit beings. Specifically he prayed, "Until the succession of one thousand buddhas of the fortunate aeon has come to an end, may my emanations appear without interruption, accomplishing vast benefit for beings to be tamed!" Accordingly, he appeared as Shariputra, one of the Buddha Shakyamuni's foremost disciples; as the prodigy translator Drogban Khye'uchung Lotsawa; and as Dampa Desheg, who founded the great Kat'hog Monastery in Eastern Tibet.

His incarnation as Dudjom Lingpa manifested in response to the explicit command of Guru Rinpoche, who ex-
horted an emanation to appear as his direct emissary in order to protect beings in these times of spiritual degeneration.
He was conceived amid wondrous signs, and at his birth in a
small felt tent, the environment was filled with rainbows and
delightful fragrances, and a rain of blossoms fell.
Embodiment in nirmanakaya form did not hinder his
complete realization of the three kayas, and through his pure
vision he had access to the wisdom of the enlightened ones
in other realms. Many of his visionary experiences are richly
recorded in *Buddhahood Without Meditation* (*Nang-jang*). He
also revealed twenty-two volumes of teachings and practices,
treasures (*terma*)* that had been hidden by Guru Rinpoche
and his consort Yeshe Tsogyal so that fresh, uncorrupted
dharma transmissions would be available to future practitioners.

The practices Dudjom Lingpa offered were so replete
with dharma potential, and the faith of his disciples so
strong, that thirteen of the disciples attained rainbow body.
At the end of his life, Dudjom Lingpa instructed his students
to go to the Padma Kod region of southeastern Tibet. They
set out, and one month later heard that their revered
teacher had passed from this realm. Having no reason to
hurry, they continued their pilgrimage for several years. At
last they arrived at a house in Padma Kod. A toddler ran
out, welcomed them by name, and invited them inside to enjoy a meal he had instructed his mother to prepare the day
before "for special guests." The little boy proved to be the incarnation of Dudjom Lingpa.

His Holiness Dudjom Jigdral Yeshe Dorje took birth
with all the qualities of his predecessor intact. He, too, was

*All italicized words in parentheses are Tibetan unless noted as San-
skrit (Skt.).

inseparable from Guru Rinpoche. Yet, just as Guru Rinpoche has eight emanations, some peaceful, some wrathful, so there were contrasts in the display of these two masters. Dudjom Lingpa embodied awesome wrath, as brilliant as lightning or an explosion of flames. Dudjom Jigdral Yeshe Dorje remained utterly peaceful—soft-spoken, charming, as refined and handsome as a peaceful male deity. Dudjom Lingpa was a supreme yogi and prodigious treasure revealer (*terton*). In Dudjom Jigdral Yeshe Dorje these qualities, though very great, were subordinated to his qualities as a scholar and teacher.

He compiled, corrected, and reprinted many old treasures, including the *Dudjom Tersar Ngondro*, and offered wonderfully lucid oral explanations and precise written commentaries. He served as a fountain of empowerments, thereby upholding the Nyingmapa lineage of Vajrayana Buddhism, which was disrupted and dangerously thin after the Chinese Communist conquest of Tibet in the 1950s. In the latter part of his life, he traveled to many countries, gathering his disciples. Indeed, he fulfilled the prophecy that whoever should see him, hear him, remember him, or be blessed by his hand would find liberation.

I had the excellent fortune to receive teachings on the *Dudjom Tersar Ngondro* directly from H.H. Dudjom Jigdral Yeshe Dorje, and at that time I made notations where his oral explanation varied somewhat from the text. These variations are slight and it would not be incorrect to practice according to the written text. However, I have incorporated the instructions from the oral explanation into my own oral instructions and into this commentary.

Although quite concise, the *Dudjom Tersar Ngondro* provides an extremely powerful practice for turning the mind toward dharma, for purification, and for bringing forth the qualities of realization. It enhances devotion to the dharma and a receptivity to the highest level of teachings. I require the *Tersar* or some other ngondro practice for my students who aspire to receive transmission of the mind teachings of Great Perfection (Dzogchen). These days lamas sometimes offer the Great Perfection teachings to those who have not undertaken ngondro. This I have grave doubts about. Until students have purified their minds and developed receptivity through the two accumulations—of merit and pristine awareness—and until they have established a profound level of guru yoga, the direct mind-to-mind transmission of Great Perfection cannot take place. Although practitioners do exist who attain realization as soon as the Great Perfection teachings fall upon their ears, they are ones who have rendered their minds completely receptive in past lives. Such practitioners may sit down, listen to the teachings, and stand up totally transformed by the spiritual perspective of Great Perfection.

Most people must develop their practice step by step, beginning with ngondro. Unless they have ripened their minds through practice, the oral transmission that should lead to a state beyond concept leads instead to more concepts. If students who could benefit from the Great Perfection teachings hear them too early, the teachings do not have the impact they otherwise would. For this reason I require ngondro before the full presentation of Great Perfection.

Some years ago a student, having assured me that he had fulfilled the ngondro requirements, attended a six-week Great Perfection retreat. As the retreat progressed, this student frequently asked questions that made no sense in the context of the teachings. He seemed impervious to my transmission. No light shone from his eyes. One day I confronted him: "I think you didn't do much ngondro." Defensive, he again assured me that he had. I regretted his reply because obviously he had locked himself into a lie. For him, retreat ended sourly, and I did not hear from him for some time afterward—not until he called to tell me that it was true that he had not completed his ngondro requirement, though he was now working on it. I felt the relief parents feel when their child levels with them on an important issue.

However, for practitioners with receptive minds, the Great Perfection perspective can evolve from ngondro itself. Its essence can be glimpsed each time the mind rests in intrinsic awareness (*rigpa*), in each experience of the absolute nature of Vajrasattva and the absolute lama in guru yoga. The *Dudjom Tersar Ngondro*—concise, unelaborate, and grounded in guru yoga—provides a superb means to open the door to recognizing the nature of mind. I hope that all who undertake it will transcend the rigors of the practices and find true joy in them.

His Holiness Dudjom Jigdral Yeshe Dorje

NGONDRO: THE FOUNDATION

Ngondro provides the foundation for all Buddhist practice until enlightenment. The Buddha taught eighty-four thousand methods of taming the mind. We would have difficulty listening to eighty-four thousand different teachings, let alone applying them as practices. Ngondro condenses the essence of all of these into a few practices that are relatively easy to accomplish and profoundly transformative. The meditative realization gained through ngondro continues as an integral support of practice, particularly Vajrayana practice. In this respect the preliminaries resemble the alphabet, which is not simply learned and cast aside, but is utilized constantly as the basis of all written communication.

The Tibetan word *ngondro* means "to go before" or "preliminary," and these preliminary practices fall into two basic categories. The first, that of the outer preliminaries, common to both the Hinayana and Mahayana Buddhist paths, consists of contemplation of the four thoughts that turn the mind. Then there are the extraordinary preliminaries special to the Mahayana and Vajrayana paths: refuge, bodhicitta, mandala offerings, Vajrasattva purification, guru yoga, and transference of consciousness.

The vehicles (Skt. *yanas*) of Hinayana, Mahayana, and Vajrayana evolved from the Buddha's teachings to meet the

1

different needs of practitioners according to their individual capabilities. At the Hinayana level, weariness with the suffering of cyclic existence (Skt. *samsara*) leads to renunciation of worldly attachments and care in maintaining moral discipline. Practitioners hope that they as individuals will find liberation from samsara and achieve the peace of nirvana.

Mahayana practitioners likewise see cyclic existence as an ocean of suffering and long for liberation, but they recognize that countless others are also helplessly foundering and drowning in samsara. Compassion wells forth and, with it, the powerful wish to alleviate their suffering. Liberation for themselves alone cannot satisfy the spiritual aspirations of Mahayana practitioners. They vow to benefit all others through their practice of the Buddhist path and to attain enlightenment in order to lead them to ultimate liberation.

Vajrayana subsumes both Hinayana and Mahayana, particularly the Mahayana commitment to lead all beings to enlightenment. Vajrayana, however, cultivates ongoing recognition of the mind as both the source of suffering and the source of liberation. Although mind is the source of the entire spectrum of experience, if we look for mind itself we cannot find it. Mind's actual nature is emptiness. We cannot point to any substantial entity and say, "That is mind." At the same time, we cannot deny the phenomena that arise in the mind, the continual experience of emotions, thoughts, and perceptions. Mind's nature remains beyond limiting concepts of existence or nonexistence. For the Vajrayana practitioner, this means that all experience is viewed as inseparable from its source, mind's pure, empty nature. Thus, whatever arises is perceived as a sacred display of pure appearances.

Practice of the outer and the extraordinary preliminaries provides a strong foundation for spiritual development. The teachings on the four thoughts give rise to the renunciation of ordinary attachments and guide us toward what is benefi-

cial. Refuge creates a sense of protection and blessing. Bodhicitta clarifies our motivation and arouses our compassion—
we acknowledge our highest spiritual aspirations. Mandala
offerings generate the accumulation of merit and the revelation of pristine awareness that we will need to fulfill our
aspirations. Vajrasattva provides a method by which we can
purify the obstacles to enlightenment—the mind's poisons,
habitual patterns, negative karma, and intellectual obscurations. Guru yoga enables us to receive the pure qualities of
the lama's realization. Transference of consciousness allows
us to continue our path uninterrupted after this lifetime by
finding rebirth in the pureland.

As we undertake ngondro, we acquire certain skills that
we will use again and again in Vajrayana practice. We learn
to contemplate, to develop a visualization, to recite prayers
and mantra, to perform prostrations and mandala offerings,
to dissolve the visualization, and to rest in nonconceptual
meditation. We begin our practice with pure motivation, follow the lineage instructions in each section, redirect our attention whenever it wanders, and close with the pure dedication of virtue to all sentient beings.

In general we learn how to meditate. Meditation means
directing the mind, training it by repetition until it complies
with our highest spiritual intentions. At first, hindered by
mental poisons, habits, and obscurations, we must exert
great effort. But once we have freed ourselves from tangles
and confusion, meditation becomes effortless and carries
over from formal practice into daily life, from day into night,
from one life to another. No moment exists apart from the
enriching revelation of meditation.

However, most practitioners find ngondro rigorous,
strenuous, sometimes frustrating. Even to begin ngondro, we
must have some measure of faith in the Buddhist path. Practice itself increases faith, which in turn carries us through all

3

the challenges ngondro poses. Faith is an unsurpassed quality for a spiritual practitioner. Initially it may awaken when we hear some fragment of a teaching, when we see a lama or an image. The mind is momentarily jolted out of its ordinary habits and experiences a freshness, a clarity and joy. This first level of faith is called "clear faith."

If that first awakening propels one into spiritual practice, faith will deepen through the transformative experience of hearing the teachings and applying them. This is called "deep faith." Someone who sincerely contemplates and meditates on the dharma usually feels positive changes day by day, or certainly week by week. These changes include a lessening of the mind's poisons and habitual tendencies, as well as increased compassion for others and a clearer perspective.

The faith that develops when we fully rely on spirituality to guide our lives is called "irreversible faith." Once such faith develops, we will not turn back no matter what obstacles arise on the path. Actually, since our practice becomes stronger in the face of obstacles, we may no longer fear obstacles or even feel an aversion to them. We acquire confidence that we can transform whatever life brings us into an opportunity for spiritual growth.

In classical Vajrayana practice, the student, inspired by some facet of Buddhism, would approach a qualified lama and request teachings. The lama would first explain contemplation of the four thoughts. If this contemplation succeeded in ripening the student's interest in dharma, the student would next ask for refuge and bodhisattva vows. These would be followed by teachings on ngondro, empowerments for Vajrasattva and Guru Rinpoche, and an oral transmission in which the lama would read the practice in Tibetan so that the blessing of the words fell on the student's ears.

Upon completing the ngondro, the student would be examined by the lama, who, if satisfied, would give the student empowerment (*wang*), oral transmission (*lung*), and teachings (*tri*) for the practice of a special meditational deity (*yidam*). Other empowerments would follow, and when the lama felt the student's mind had been sufficiently ripened through blessing and practice, the empowerment and oral transmission for Great Perfection practice would be offered. Great Perfection transmission pivots on the accomplishment of guru yoga. The term "guru yoga" literally means "union with the nature of the guru," and through the practice we blend our own mind with the enlightened mind of the lama. Guru yoga surpasses every other method as a direct, exalted means to reach enlightenment. All buddhas in the past relied on a spiritual teacher to achieve buddhahood; all buddhas in the future will likewise do so. Both unwavering devotion for the teacher and recognition that the teacher's qualities are no different from those of an enlightened buddha signal mastery of guru yoga. Ultimately, the blessing of guru yoga expresses itself through full transmission from the lama's enlightened mind to the student's mind.

In ngondro, guru yoga follows prostrations, mandala offerings, and Vajrasattva, but the key points can be incorporated into practice from the beginning. By seeing our teacher as inseparable from Guru Rinpoche, Vajrasattva, and Buddha Amitabha, and by blending our mind nondually with the teacher's upon the dissolution of visualizations, we greatly enhance the power of our practice. Each section of the ngondro becomes a preparation for the consummate guru yoga practices of the Great Perfection. Much more detailed explanations of these points follow.

INVOCATION

The first line of the ngondro invokes the lama with "*Namo*," which means "homage," and continues, "O lama, infallible constant protector." The title "lama" represents the attainment of specific spiritual qualities that infallibly protect and benefit sentient beings. An authentic lama holds an unbroken lineage of the Buddha's teachings. He or she has studied the teachings, contemplated them, and questioned them until all doubts have been thoroughly resolved and clear comprehension has dawned. Going beyond a scholarly, intellectual approach, the lama has meditated until the very essence of the teachings—particularly those concerning bodhicitta and the nature of mind—has wrought profound transformation. Bodhicitta motivation inspires the lama to lead beings out of the pit of samsara. With the lama's realization of emptiness, compassion and love benefit beings spontaneously and the lama's blessings penetrate their mindstreams. For this reason it is said that if we see, hear, remember, or touch the lama we can find liberation. The lama's compassion always connects with our devotion, like the linking of a hook and an eye.

The intellectual understanding acquired through scholarly endeavors represents a necessary and valuable component of a lama's training. However, we would not want to rely spiritually on someone who has studied books but not integrated their meaning through meditation any more than we would trust a surgeon who is a brilliant theoretician but has never performed an operation or a driving instructor who knows the rules of the road but does not in fact drive. We seek a lama who has attained the open perspective of a meditator, who can see beyond the ordinary patterns of phenomena, who can guide our meditation with his or her own. Many experiences can arise in meditation, some positive and some disturbing. The lama has meditated until he or she has obtained confidence in all levels of practice, and can discriminate between mere transitory meditative phenomena and stable signs of attainment. From experience gained in meditation, the lama can guide us around pitfalls in our own meditation and inspire us to the highest spiritual accomplishment. A qualified lama helps us develop the sequence of our training, enhancing current practices or changing emphasis when appropriate so we follow the most direct path to realization. A single type of meditation may not be the most effective way to train our mind, any more than a single medicine will cure all the illnesses that may afflict us over an extended period. Vajrayana methods vary according to the personality and capabilities of practitioners as well as the types of obstacles they encounter. The lama provides us with the skillful means to deal with our individual circumstances and mentalities.

The lama's training also protects us because it refines our sense of what conduct of body, speech, and mind to accept and what to reject. We avoid planting karmic seeds for future suffering, and in this sense the lama offers us constant protection in this life and future lives. The lama's prayers and guidance can also protect us from the obstacles arising from past karma. Though we may still be confronted by difficult situations, the lama shows us how to work with them through our practice.

Our connection with an infallible lama indicates great merit and strong prayers of aspiration in past lives. However, a terrible spiritual tragedy results if we meet and follow a false teacher who distorts the teachings and does not base spiritual instruction on pure lineage transmission, who merely pretends to have realization, whose concern for followers is motivated by self-interest. Such teachers waste their followers' opportunity for spiritual development in this life, betray them when they die, and undermine the merit they need to find a spiritual path in the future. If treated by an incompetent, fraudulent physician, a patient can expect declining health or a loss of life. If guided by a false teacher, a student can expect to lose spiritual well-being for this and many lifetimes to come.

Some enlightened lamas manifest wisdom in unconventional ways; some charlatan lamas seem serene and wise and have fine reputations. How can we know the difference? We check their lineage—true lamas revere their lineage and have served their own teachers with exemplary devotion. We check their motivation, their good heart. Is their intention really to benefit sentient beings? Can we feel compassion underlying their actions? Again, wrathful activity can be carried out with unconditional love and compassion; peacefulness can be hypocritical. We check back. Do we experience a greater clarity as a result of the lama's words and actions? Are our mind's workings illuminated? Do we gather impetus to practice and correct our conduct? A true lama can bring about moments of positive transformation through the skillful means of dharma. A false lama merely manipulates our spirituality and reinforces poisonous emotions and deluded tendencies. Someone posing as a lama, but devoid of pure

lineage and pure motivation, devoid of the qualities that
arise from authentic meditation, resembles something foul
wrapped in brocade. The eye may be deceived, but the nose
can smell it.

Once we have found an infallible lama, we should hold
him or her as dear as our own breath. Now we have access
to a treasury of spiritual attainment. In our interactions, we
try to see the lama through less ordinary eyes, cultivating the
pure view that the lama's activities of body, speech, and
mind remain inseparable from Guru Rinpoche. Although in
a relative way we might find fault with the lama's human
foibles, this tendency to belittle and criticize undermines
our own spiritual development. The lama has intentionally
accepted the limitations and suffering of human rebirth, yet
abides in the recognition of buddha nature. Outwardly, to
guide us, the lama may act like one of us; actually, he or she
is completely different. If our obscurations make us too near-
sighted to perceive the buddha manifestation in the lama's
outer display, at least we must refrain from any immature,
arrogant judgments. Otherwise we may block our avenue of
liberation.

A Western student recently wrote of an encounter with
his lama, the late Chogyam Trungpa Rinpoche, an irrefut-
able realization holder and a famous drinker. Sitting on a
balcony, Trungpa Rinpoche signaled this student to come up
and help him to his room. As he supported Trungpa Rinpoche, the student caught a whiff of alcohol. When they entered the room, Trungpa turned and said, "I understand
you have been having trouble meditating." He gestured
toward some pillows. "Sit here and meditate for me."

As the student sat down, a thought crossed his mind:
"What can this drunken person do for my meditation?"
Later he recollected, "After a bit I could feel him in my head
cutting this bind, untying this knot, and releasing this staple

until the top of my head floated free, and I had three-hundred-sixty-degree vision."

When the student bowed to take leave, Trungpa Rinpoche advised, "Always separate the man from the teacher."

The historical Buddha Shakyamuni faultlessly demonstrated the path to enlightenment, but at present he is not accessible to us. In the sense that our lama has willingly taken human rebirth to guide and protect us on the path, he or she shows us more direct kindness than even the Buddha. We can respond to the lama's matchless kindness with material support, by using our skills and energy to carry out his or her activity, and through the accomplishment of spiritual practice. Although meditating until signs of accomplishment arise certainly represents the highest mode of service, the great practitioners before us, honoring the priceless treasure of their lamas' teachings and empowerments, have unstintingly made offerings on all levels.

Lamas can be delineated into six categories, although a single lama may serve the functions of all six. First, the general lama (*kyü lopon*) gives us vows of refuge and bodhicitta as well as basic teachings. General lamas may hold many lineages or only one, but they have always received the authorization to teach what they know. Second, the vajra regent (*dorje gyaltsab*) ripens our mind for empowerment. Third, the empowerment lama (*wanggi lopon*) gives us empowerments into the levels of maha, anu, and ati yoga. Merely attending the ceremony does not constitute empowerment. Rather, empowerment depends on what takes place inwardly, in the depths of our mind—whether we achieve realization, attain meditational states of bliss, clarity, and emptiness, or gain wisdom recognition of vajra body, speech, and mind. If none of these signs occur, we may have received blessings, but not full empowerment.

Fourth is the lama who witnesses our purification when

11

vows and commitments have been damaged (*nyam chhag kangwai lopon*). Fifth is the lama who teaches us what to accept and what to reject on the Vajrayana path (*shey gyud drolwai lopon*). Sixth is the lama who fosters our main practice, who leads us through the stages of development and completion, who instills in our mindstream the transmission of intrinsic awareness (*rigpa*), and who is revered as our root lama, the lama of direct oral transmission (*man-ngag lungi lopon*).

The process of recognizing that our mind and the mind of our root lama are in essence inseparable constitutes the shortest path to enlightenment. This depends, however, on our overcoming all the barriers that our ego erects between us and our teacher. In ngondro, each time we visualize the teacher as inseparable from the deity—from Guru Rinpoche, Vajrasattva, Amitabha—and each time we dissolve the visualization into light, which is absorbed into our own form, and then rest nondually in the single absolute nature of our mind and the lama's, we come closer to realization of the absolute lama. Any practice that brings us to this realization—whether it is in the context of ngondro, a deity practice, or Great Perfection—serves the highest purpose of Vajrayana Buddhism.

THE OUTER
PRELIMINARIES

FOUR CONTEMPLATIONS THAT
CHANGE THE MIND:
AN OVERVIEW

Contemplation of the four thoughts that change the mind follows the invocation. For those who have not taken refuge, these four contemplations are the threshold of the Buddhist path; through them, we explore both the personal relevance and universal meaning of Buddhist doctrine. After we enter the door of refuge, these reflections constantly strengthen and renew our practice. Contemplation of precious human birth and impermanence inspires a deep renunciation of the limiting concerns of this lifetime; contemplation of karma and suffering brings a renunciation of cyclic existence altogether.

The saintly lama Tulku Arig, who lived in the Tromt'har region of Eastern Tibet, always emphasized the four contemplations in his teachings. He spent his whole life in retreat, until his death in 1987 at the age of eighty-three. When the Chinese came, they did not harass him as much as they did other lamas, because he had so few possessions and always lived in a tent, hut, or cave. Also, on the various occasions when they did send people to badger him, these people could not sustain their hostility in the presence of Tulku Arig's purity. If they came back several times, their minds would turn with faith toward Tulku Arig, rendering them useless as subversives for the Chinese.

Because he was in retreat, opportunities to receive teachings from him were rare. He could teach at any level, from the sutras to the highest Great Perfection, but for years he chose to teach the four thoughts. Those who grasped at what they regarded as higher levels of Vajrayana pleaded with him to move on to other teachings. He adamantly refused, saying, "The lineage lamas before me meditated for years and years to understand the full meaning of the doctrines. If this teaching, which was worthy of those lamas, is not deep enough for you, you should go someplace else. I don't have any teachings deep enough for you."

Teachings on the four contemplations—precious human birth, impermanence, karma, and suffering—provide an overview of forces and conditions that create our experience within cyclic existence. As background to the four thoughts, however, it is useful to know something about the six intermediate states (*bardos*) that actually comprise a "cycle" in cyclic existence.

The six bardos include four transitory states during our lifetime and two between death and rebirth. The first, the birthplace bardo (*kye nay bardo*), spans the moment of birth to the moment we encounter the conditions that will result in our death. The second, the moment-of-death bardo (*chhikhai bardo*), may be a sustained moment, as in the case of a lengthy terminal illness, or an instant, as in a sudden accident. Either way, this bardo leads irreversibly to death. During these two bardos that bridge birth and death, the dream bardo (*milam bardo*) and bardo of meditative concentration (*samtan bardo*) also occur. After death, one's consciousness recovers from a deep swoon and awakens into the bardo of the true nature of reality (*chhönyid bardo*)—first to the experience of clear, unobstructed awareness, then to the display of the peaceful and wrathful deities. Finally, the mind moves into the bardo of becoming (*sridpai bardo*), where it

16

sheathes itself in a mental body and, amid turbulent projections of its karma, moves toward its destined rebirth and another cycle of existence. The mind has circled ceaselessly in this way since the beginningless beginning.

How successfully we deal with each of these bardo transitions depends on what we accomplish spiritually in the birthplace bardo—that is, in our lives now. Accomplishment can start with contemplation of the four thoughts. By thoroughly reflecting on impermanence, for example, we recognize that everything fluctuates, that stability is just an illusion, and that seemingly solid appearances have no inherent reality. This knowledge undercuts attachment; and attachment—to people, to possessions, to our own bodies—acts as a terrible hindrance when we enter the moment-of-death bardo. To the extent that we train ourselves to see everything as impermanent, we free our minds from attachment and face death with much less suffering. Thus, impermanence, only a concept to explore at the outset of our spiritual path, becomes a perspective that serves us well as we approach death.

Contemplation of impermanence and the illusory quality of appearances also represents our first step toward mastery of the dream bardo and the goal of uninterrupted meditation while dreaming. Contemplation of karma instills an urgency to purify our karma now, before we become completely vulnerable to hallucinatory karmic projections in the bardo of becoming. Reflecting on our precious human birth reminds us not to waste this rare, hard-earned opportunity lest the wheel of samsara turn and thrust us into a different, much less auspicious birthplace bardo. Contemplation is an important aspect of training in meditation. Focusing thoughts, reining them in when they take off on a tangent, plunging them into the topic of contemplation, then cutting them altogether and resting in nonconceptual meditation—these skills prepare us for the bardo of meditative concentration in this life and the bardo of the true nature of reality after death.

In reflecting on the four thoughts, we alternate contemplation with resting the mind in nonconceptual meditation. As contemplation transforms inner perception, the mind's grasping at ordinary appearances relaxes and outer conditions can be seen differently as well. Then, during the phase of nonconceptual meditation, the mind's busyness, its dualistic tendency to frame everything as subject and object, self and other, begins to subside. As our sense of mind's relaxation deepens, the stage is set for the introduction of Great Perfection.

The general instructions for meditation on the four thoughts are given below; these should not limit what we consider relevant, however. We need to gain such deep, personal insight into each of these four thoughts that they become fully integrated into our day-to-day activities, informing every moment of our life. The insights and meditative realization that arise in our formal sessions change our view of ordinary events, and the events of our daily life provide grist for our contemplations. We might try contemplating impermanence while driving down the highway, for instance, or precious human birth when we are tempted to indulge some addiction, or suffering as we watch a sports event, or karma when a colleague irritates us. The lenses of the four thoughts provide a kaleidoscope of perspectives and a wealth of spiritual understanding.

MEDITATION INSTRUCTIONS

Begin by exploring the direct relevance of this sacred wisdom to your own life and to that of others. Then drop your thoughts and rest in nonconceptual meditation. Next, use the thrust of contemplation to arouse compassion, then rest the mind. Next, pray that all beings find liberation from the conditions of cyclic existence, invoking the blessing of the wisdom beings to accomplish this aspiration. Rest. Finally, renew your commitment to the path of enlightenment in order to benefit beings ceaselessly. Again, rest.

At first, spend most of your time in contemplation, thinking until you are weary of thinking. Then cut your thoughts and rest. When thoughts arise, as they always do, simply direct them into the next phase of contemplation. Some dharma practitioners try to meditate with impervious nonconceptuality in order to find a respite from the constant chatter of their minds. But as soon as they stop meditating, the chatter begins again—much as if, having pressed the pause button on a tape recorder to avoid listening to a tape, they find the music continuing as soon as they release the button. More effectively, they could change the tape altogether. Contemplation of the four thoughts changes the tape of mundane thoughts.

The spiritual insights you gather through contemplation expand into meditative realization as you rest the mind. Nothing is lost because you do not frame such insights in words. Returning to active contemplation, you will find your intellect refreshed by that moment of nonconceptual relaxation. Like a bird soaring on both wings in flight, contemplation and meditation together train the mind.

The four thoughts can be contemplated as a prelude to the other sections of the ngondro or as a practice in itself. If you make them a separate practice, open with the Seven-Line Prayer and the invocation, then close with the dedication.

PRECIOUS HUMAN BIRTH

We begin the process of developing a spiritual perspective by contemplating the precious opportunity of having a fully endowed human birth as a working basis for spiritual development. Our body can be compared to a boat, our mind to its captain. If we use them well, we can cross the treacherous currents of cyclic existence to the shores of absolute truth. To have this precious opportunity and not use it represents a great waste—as if we had traveled to an island of wish-fulfilling jewels and brought none back with us. What regret we would feel!

Such a birth represents the culmination of great virtue and fervent aspiration to pursue spiritual practice. This does not mean that it lacks difficulties or frustration. We must endure birth, sickness, old age, and death, and we often cannot get what we want, or avoid what we do not want, or keep what we have. Nevertheless, we do enjoy eighteen freedoms and favorable conditions, summed up by the Tibetan term *dal jor*—*dal* referring to freedom from eight unfavorable conditions, *jor* to endowment with ten favorable conditions.

Being endowed with the eight freedoms means being free of circumstances that make it almost impossible to connect with the dharma. These include freedom from rebirth as a hell being, deprived spirit, or animal, which entails overwhelming suffering; rebirth among the long-lived gods, which seduces us with irresistible sense pleasures (in the lower god realms) and pleasurable states of consciousness (in the upper god realms); rebirth in a vicious culture that sanctions violence and evil and cuts us off from the sacred dharma; rebirth with wrong views that cause us to demean what is sacred and wholesome and relish what is detrimental; rebirth in a dark aeon when no buddha manifests, leaving us bereft of a spiritual path; and finally, rebirth with physical and mental disabilities so severe that we cannot hear or comprehend the teachings.

The ten favorable conditions fall into two categories. The first includes conditions that correspond to one's personal situation: being born as a human being, living in a place where the dharma can be found, having all one's faculties, having refrained from heinous crimes (such as wounding a buddha, killing a parent, or causing a major schism in the sangha), and having confidence in the moral doctrine of the Buddha as the foundation of all positive qualities. The second category includes conditions that define the general context in which spiritual development can occur: the appearance of a buddha in the world, the teaching of the doctrine, the enduring quality of the doctrine, the opportunity to practice the teachings, and the presence of teachers whose altruistic compassion and love support one's spiritual endeavors.

The extreme difficulty of finding rebirth in the human realm, fully endowed with all freedoms and favorable conditions, is indicated by certain metaphors. For example, the number of hell beings in proportion to human beings is said to be like the number of particles of dirt on this earth compared with the particles of dirt under a fingernail. The number of human beings indifferent to spirituality in proportion to those who seek it is compared to the multiplicity of night stars contrasted with the rarity of daytime stars, and among spiritual seekers, those who practice seriously are that much rarer still.

Another way of thinking about the difficulty of finding human rebirth involves the image of the entire universe as one vast ocean. On the surface of that ocean floats a yoke tossed by the winds and currents, and in the depths of that ocean swims a blind sea turtle who surfaces only once in a century. The chance of one's finding human rebirth equals the probability that the blind sea turtle surfacing after a hundred years will poke its head through the yoke in the universal ocean.

Westerners often believe that one takes rebirth after rebirth as a human being, and they tend to regard their past lives as a fascinating series of adventures just beyond the reach of memory. Really, though, we all have had endless varieties of rebirths from the beginningless beginning of existence, each of them an exact reflection of our karma and few of them as human beings.

Our body represents a composite entity that disintegrates into dust at death. Mind is substanceless, but has powerful continuity. Both its immutable nature and its karmic tendencies continue through cycles of death and rebirth. We need only survey the thoughts that arise in our mind to see that just a fraction of them are of the sort that create the fortunate karma to obtain a fully endowed human birth. Most thoughts are tainted with attachment and aversion. Even subtle mental poisons can undercut an auspicious rebirth, but the worst thoughts, those filled with violent hatred, may propel us toward rebirth in hell.

Patrul Rinpoche clearly understood the subtle connection between thoughts, karma, and rebirth. He lived a simple, ascetic life, often traveling about, never taking much with him, listening to teachings from many lamas. Sometimes these lamas had no idea that the humble monk who listened so intently to their discourses was the renowned scholar Patrul Rinpoche, because he did not announce his name or display his status as one of the most revered lamas of his generation.

One day he stopped in a meadow. As he rested, enjoying the blue sky overhead and the carpet of flowers that covered the land, he thought, "How beautiful it is." In the next instant he added, "May I not be reborn here." He later explained that attachment to its beauty might have led to rebirth in that place, possibly as an animal, perhaps even as an insect, since there were no human inhabitants.

If we deeply contemplate its preciousness, we will be inspired to make good use of our human birth with its unsurpassed potential for enlightenment. Taking it for granted will be a cause for immeasurable sorrow. We must train our mind in the time remaining and clear away untamed thoughts before they proliferate into the countless forms of samsara.

MEDITATION INSTRUCTIONS

First, contemplate the importance of having a precious human birth endowed with all the freedoms and conditions necessary for spiritual practice. How rare! How uncertain it is that you will find it again, since the mind could easily lead you into a nonhuman realm or into a human birth without full endowment. Reflect on how great your virtue and aspiration must have been previously for you to have gathered these present fortunate conditions. Contemplate until the exceptional opportunity afforded by this life, not to be taken for granted or wasted, becomes clearly apparent. Then allow the mind to rest in natural, nonconceptual meditation.

When thoughts arise, direct them toward compassion. Consider those suffering in lower realms who have little possibility of obtaining a human rebirth because dense obscurations prevent them from generating merit. Think of those who have a human body but who are not endowed with conditions conducive to spiritual development. Reflect on those who attain a human birth but squander it on worldly pursuits or destroy their opportunity by harming others. Remember that, even for practitioners, the tenure of this lifetime remains as uncertain as that of a candle flame in the wind. When contemplation leads to the deep-seated wish that all beings find liberation from spiritually impoverished circumstances, relax the mind.

When thoughts arise, pray to the lama as the embodiment of the buddhas and bodhisattvas of the ten directions. Pray that this wish-fulfilling jewel of human birth not be thrown irretrievably into the ocean of samsara, that instead it be used well to create merit and gain recognition of mind's true nature. Pray that those suffering in other realms may find human rebirth, that those human beings not endowed with spiritual conditions may find them, that those fortunate enough to be endowed with spiritual conditions may fulfill their highest aspirations. Pray to attain the power to help them. Then rest.

Finally, as thoughts present themselves once more, direct them toward commitment. Think, "In my past lives altogether, I have had innumerable bodies, each of which I cherished, fed, and defended. If all of their corpses were piled up, they would form a mountain the size of Meru. The blood that raced through those bodies, the tears shed in frustration would form an enormous ocean. Yet in those lifetimes I failed to accomplish enlightenment. Now, through the accumulation of all my merit, I have attained this one extraordinary birth. This I will use well, for the greatest benefit of all sentient beings." Then, again, rest the mind in uncontrived meditation.

IMPERMANENCE AND DEATH

Nothing lasts, everything changes constantly, relentlessly, and no one should ever presume the permanence of anything. With each moment of our life we move closer to death, and we cannot stave it off when our time finally comes. We will die, our loved ones will die, all beings born in the six realms will die. Only the time of death remains uncertain, and where and how. Death itself is inevitable.

Most people live in denial of death; practitioners live in unflinching mindfulness. Death for them is a powerful directive to find the essential meaning of life. In Tibetan Vajrayana practice, the symbols of death—skullcups, skull drums, thighbone trumpets, bone malas, dancers in skeleton costumes—vividly remind one of the immediacy of death. The use of such implements during rituals does not mean that Vajrayana practitioners are callous to death or do not grieve over the deaths of family members and friends, but the smell and texture of old bones, for example, evoke the thought "Yes, I, too, will end up as scattered bones or ashes in a cremation ground. May I use this body well and not waste the time I have left!"

In the West almost every time we turn on the television or pick up a newspaper or a magazine, our mind is invaded by images of death—deaths in the thousands brought on by natural catastrophes or wars, deaths of famous public figures, deaths of ordinary people who die suddenly in strange circumstances. Yet it is unusual to find anyone who has really integrated the inescapable reality of death into their perspective on life. Few are prepared. They see clouds gathering on the horizon but always expect the storm to break elsewhere.

Of the four reflections, the contemplation of death and impermanence is the most powerful spur to practice. Death and impermanence are not two forces; death is the dramatic display of impermanence. In truth, every phenomenon is a continuum of change, a series of infinitesimal deaths whereby what exists in one instant ceases to be in the next.

On a subatomic level the densest iron bar constantly decays and becomes restructured—our mind's subtle perception can pierce its apparent solidity. On an inconceivably vast scale, the universe has arisen from emptiness and will disperse into emptiness. When this world has been consumed by fire seven times, drenched by water once, and scattered by wind, it will disappear. Mount Meru, the center of the cosmos, resplendent with jewels and precious metals, will give way to the forces of impermanence. Meanwhile, stars explode, the seasons change, days become nights, and our possessions, relationships, thoughts, and emotions come and go in a ceaseless, ever-mutable display.

Shakyamuni Buddha demonstrated impermanence by his own passing into parinirvana. His disciples, as well as great saints and teachers, translators and scholars, dharma kings and upholders of the doctrine whose names and brilliant accomplishments illuminated their own time, exist only in stories or are forgotten to us now. Many of the Buddhist monuments that once adorned India, Afghanistan, Pakistan, China, Cambodia, Vietnam, and Indonesia have been reduced to heaps of ruble, desecrated ruins, and broken statues.

In Tibet, many monasteries where thousands of monks practiced are now devastated, the sacred texts destroyed, the artworks stolen, and great teachers killed or growing old in exile. Tibetan people who once herded yaks and sheep in the snow mountains now sell sweaters beside the road on the hot plains of India.

Everything in samsara is composite. As it comes together, so it falls apart. Reflect on these things and ordinary reality becomes but a series of dreamlike appearances, mirages, bubbles. Whether those appearances bring joy or sorrow, we need not grasp at them—they are not reliable, permanent, inherently true. Yet we cannot deny our experience of their ceaseless display. Thoroughly exploring the nature of impermanence eventually brings us to a view beyond the extremes of existence and nonexistence, a view of appearances inseparable from their own empty nature.

MEDITATION INSTRUCTIONS

First, contemplate impermanence—the progression from birth to old age and death, people who have come and gone, possessions, shifting scenery, the kaleidoscopic play of phenomena. Think about the universe in constant motion; think about the subatomic particles of your own body, so kinetic that in any instant their existence and whereabouts are only a probability. Contemplate death, the countless deaths before and the countless deaths yet to come, the uncertainty of when and how death will happen next. Imagine specific ways death might occur, the sudden severance from friends and family. Contemplate until you perceive the seeming cohesion of life as a transparent illusion. When weary of contemplation, rest the mind.

When thoughts arise, direct them toward compassion. Reflect on how we usually live in denial of impermanence, yet are undercut again and again when what we relied on as solid and enduring disintegrates and disappears. Remember the suffering at the moment of death—the fear, the separation from loved ones and possessions—and remember the tumultuous experiences in the bardo after death. Think how most beings, oblivious to impermanence, lose their sense of priority. Reflect in this way until compassion for them surges forth, then rest, beyond concept.

Again, when mind's incessant creativity gives rise to thoughts, direct them toward prayer, that all beings may attain such profound realization of impermanence that it totally purifies the tendency to hold to appearances as real, as well as all attachment and aversion that stem from that holding. Pray that you may go through death's transitions maintaining recognition of mind's nature and that your realization will become so strong that you can rescue others from the turmoil of the bardo. Then rest the mind.

Finally, when thoughts present themselves, formulate the commitment to live and practice in unwavering cognizance of impermanence. Commit yourself to realizing the true nature of all phenomena, positive or negative, and to searching for the absolute essence. With this resolve, relax in uncontrived meditation.

KARMA

Our actions—virtuous and nonvirtuous, white and black—weave the patterns of our experience in samsara. Whether we encounter pleasure or pain, or reach the heights or the depths of cyclic existence, is determined by the quality of our own conduct over countless past lifetimes. Karma is the inevitable outflow of results from causes.

By understanding the forces of karma, by purifying negativity, and by bringing our conduct into accord with what is positive, we establish a powerful spiritual compass that will serve us until we reach the very threshold of enlightenment. An enlightened buddha has passed beyond karmic dualism to attain an infinitely positive state so radiant that even its reflection can awaken our experience of buddha nature. We ourselves aspire to that exalted state, but the path to the absolute revelation of buddha nature requires assiduous attention to karma. As Guru Rinpoche himself said, "Though my view is as high as the sky, my discernment of correct conduct is as fine as barley flour."

Over countless lifetimes, each sentient being weaves a karmic web so extensive that the full pattern cannot be perceived. Many people live in dread because of unknown karmic forces, suffering all sorts of unexplained fears and phobias. To overcome bewilderment and fear, to purify old karma and create desirable conditions, we must acknowledge that our situation results from our own actions. Acknowledgment brings a certain freedom, because we no longer attribute what befalls us to forces beyond our control, to some powerful god or demon who out of wrath sends forth afflictions, or out of sublime indifference grants no respite from our suffering. What we created, we can change.

Our karmic creations resemble a forgotten play we wrote long ago. Suddenly we find it taking place on stage and ourselves starring in the drama. We wrote the lead part and even cast the characters, and the play's episodes of joy or sorrow unfold according to the script we created. One after another, the scenes must be enacted, and it's too late to change the performance. Our sole recourse is to write a different play for the future.

Karmic creation has its source in the mind, with speech and body following mind's lead. Mind's dualistic delusion fosters the tendency to fixate on desires, to become frustrated and angry if these desires are thwarted, to become proud if desires find fulfillment, to become jealous if they are fulfilled for someone else. Lost in its own projections, the mind becomes duller and less discriminating about cause and effect. Thus, a secondary stupidity arises from fundamental ignorance of the nondual nature of existence.

Positive actions accord with virtue—with altruism, kindness, patience, generosity, correct conduct, and so forth. The mind and activities of a virtuous person become more refined, less self-centered, less stupid, and less apt to cause either deliberate or accidental harm.

A common question pertains to the relationship between individual karma and group karma. Genocide represents an extreme example, in that a whole segment of the population, including children who in their short lifetime have surely done no serious wrongdoing, is threatened with annihilation.

Swept up in such overwhelming circumstances, how could any individual acknowledge genocide as his or her individual karmic creation?

The fact is that even the hideous injustice of genocide reflects the karma of each victim. Each has the karmic destiny to be part of the group's suffering. Some, according to their karma, will die; some will not. Some will sustain their humanity and compassion, some will become completely debased—even in the impersonal leveling of mass murder, each person has his or her own inner experience. If, in such a terrible situation, one feels compassion for others in a similar predicament, profound purification of karma takes place.

A story is told of Shakyamuni Buddha's life, countless rebirths before, in hell. He and another tormented being had the agonizing task of dragging a chariot up a steep mountainside, passing through a gauntlet of the minions of hell, who cudgeled and whipped them and relentlessly prodded them when they collapsed. This brutality and the unbearable conditions of hell—the flames licking their skin, the molten lava flowing over their feet, the hot winds searing their lungs—made dying preferable, but they could not escape through death. Each time it seemed their bodies would disintegrate, instead they revived. Centuries of torture stretched into thousands of years; futile cycles of pulling the chariot up, then letting it roll down, multiplied beyond counting.

One day as the buddha-to-be watched his fallen partner being savaged, his heart was moved to sudden compassion. "Let him be!" he cried. "It is useless for both him and me to endure this. I will pull the chariot alone."

Instantly the guardians of hell riveted their menace on him. "Fool!" one of them bellowed. "You dare tell us what to do? You will take his punishment, not his task!" They set upon him with unprecedented fury, beating him until, miraculously, he died. His single moment of compassion was enough to purify the karma that might have bound him to hell for aeons. In all his lifetimes thereafter that compassion constantly expanded, first into the immense compassion of a bodhisattva and then into the boundless compassion of a buddha.

One moment of pain, even a headache, in the human realm purifies karma that would cause centuries of anguish in hell, because we can transform suffering by cultivating a spiritual perspective. If we use adversity as a catalyst for compassion and virtue, karmic purification becomes swift and profound. On the other hand, if we try to improve the outer circumstances of adversity while ignoring the karmic causes, we sometimes find them intractable. Treating a karmically caused illness illustrates this.

Ultimately all sickness stems from karma. What we term "karmically caused illness" differs from ordinary illness, however, in that it does not respond to treatment, or if it does, a new disease soon replaces it. Medicines that work for others prove ineffective, and one affliction after another undermines one's well-being. If one seeks spiritual guidance because the doctors have failed, a lama might suggest doing purification practice or saving the lives of others (bait worms or shrimp, for example). After some practice, one might finally find the right medical treatment, or the illness might simply abate with no other treatment. With very stubborn illnesses or in terminal cases, purification practice offers reassurance that in future lifetimes one will not confront the results of that same karma.

Some years ago, a woman in Switzerland opened her private interview with Chagdud Rinpoche by stating, "I have cancer. Two operations have failed to cure it, and now I am going to die." She said this with no emotion whatsoever and Rinpoche did not contradict her. He only suggested that purifying karma would benefit her preparations for death.

She accepted this, so he gave her a Red Tara practice, and a generous Swiss student offered her a place to do retreat for a month or two. Rinpoche never saw her again, but later learned that she did indeed do a very diligent retreat, that all of her symptoms disappeared and she lived on for years.

In delineating what to abandon and what to accept, Buddhist doctrine categorizes karma into the ten nonvirtues and ten virtues.

THE TEN NONVIRTUES

The ten nonvirtues include three of body—killing, stealing, and sexual misconduct; four of speech—lying, slander, harsh speech, and idle talk; and three of mind—covetousness, malice, and wrong view. Three categories of karmic results—obvious experience, experience similar to the cause, and tendencies similar to the cause—ripen from our actions. A thief being reborn in the deprived spirit realm illustrates the obvious experience of karmic results. A thief being reborn as a human who is preyed upon by thieves exemplifies experience similar to the cause, while a thief being reborn as a human with a strong instinct to steal personifies tendencies similar to the cause.

Of all nonvirtues, killing is the most terrible, and of the various reasons for taking life, killing in a premeditated way out of anger and hatred is the worst, leading to rebirth in hell. Killing out of desire, such as killing for meat, fur, or possessions, can lead to rebirth as a deprived spirit. Killing out of ignorance or carelessness can lead to rebirth as an animal. If the karma of having killed another has not fully ripened or if it has been partially mitigated in previous lifetimes, then the murderer might be born in a high realm yet have much sickness, a short life, and possibly a violent death or be born into a dangerous or drab environment.

Stealing means taking what has not been given. Related to stealing are the use of our authority to coerce others to hand over their property (as when a despot taxes unfairly) or depriving through deceit (in the instance of a business-person who overcharges). Stealing can lead to rebirth as a deprived spirit or to other circumstances of extreme impoverishment.

For monks and nuns, sexual misconduct consists of violating vows of celibacy by intercourse or masturbation. Laypersons transgress through adultery. Related misconduct is incest, seduction of children or others who are taboo, rape, intercourse in a holy place or at times when one has taken a sacred vow of no sex, using prostitutes, and improper modes of sex. The outcome of sexual misconduct can be rebirth in hell, as a deprived spirit, or in filthy places, foul with excrement. At best, we end up with an ugly, quarrelsome spouse and many enemies.

Telling lies falls into three categories. Great, destructive lies are intended to change another's opinion about a sublime person or about doctrines of religious truth. Also within the category of great lies falls investing ourselves with false spiritual authority such as claiming lineage we do not have, giving wrong answers, and offering empowerments we are not authorized to give.

Ordinary lies are told at someone else's expense or in violation of their trust. We want more money so we lie about the quality of our goods; we want to avoid punishment so we lie that someone else was responsible for our own wrongdoing; we want respect so we take credit for someone else's work. Always, to some degree, ordinary lies cause harm, whereas lies of the third kind, lies of vanity, though dishonest and self-aggrandizing, deceive without harming. Here we boast of intellectual, psychic, and spiritual abilities we don't have or exaggerate our importance in various events.

Lying can result in rebirth as an animal. If born as a human, we will be slandered, verbally abused, gullible, and easily swindled. Halitosis can also result from lying.

Slander causes a rift, setting one person against another. Even if true, slanderous words that damage one person's opinion of another create nonvirtue. Similarly, because of its divisive intention, the karmic results of slander arise whether openly stated in front of the maligned person or whispered as clandestine tale-telling. Rebirth in hell will occur from slander that deliberately fosters schisms in the sangha. If born a human, we will have no friends and will encounter aggressive people who are openly contemptuous. Disagreements will flare easily, and employees will be difficult and rebellious.

Harsh speech means the use of abusive words to criticize and condemn others, and related to it are unfriendly words that humiliate. Whatever the intention, harsh speech tends to evoke hatred in another's heart. Whoever uses it will be reborn in evil circumstances, the worst being hell when the abuse has been directed toward a bodhisattva. Almost as bad is speaking hurtful words to our mother, father, or other kin. A Tibetan proverb says, "Though words may not have arrows and swords, they tear a person's heart to pieces." Even if harsh speech does not lead to rebirth in the lower realms, we may be born in a hot, stony environment among wicked people and hear unpleasant things. Whatever we say will cause quarrels.

Idle talk involves chattering unnecessarily, expounding wrong doctrines, or giving dharma instructions to someone who does not want to listen or who is not a proper vessel. At its worst, idle talk confuses someone who is ready for spiritual teaching. A related nonvirtue is speaking incoherent and indecent words. Idle talk can lead to rebirth as an animal, or if we are born a human, people disregard our words and do not respect our opinions no matter how true or sincerely spoken. An outer reflection of idle talk is the necessity of moving often because of unstable circumstances.

Covetousness is wanting to appropriate another's wealth or the wealth of natural resources. Similarly, we may covet others' qualities such as their intellect or talents. Whether we covet wealth or qualities, we take no pleasure in the fact that someone else has acquired them. The worst result of covetousness brings rebirth among the deprived spirits, but if we take rebirth as a human, we will be exceedingly greedy and possibly incontinent. Our wishes will be thwarted and we will get exactly the opposite of what we desire.

Malice means hatred and harmful intent toward others. It arises from seeing another as an enemy and harboring hostility, from seeing another as a rival and harboring envy, or from seeing another as one who has wronged us and harboring vengeance. Malice can cause rebirth in hell, but if we find rebirth as a human, we will be a spiteful person in a savage environment, a target for attacks and extremely paranoid.

Holders of wrong views deny the laws of cause and effect and refuse to acknowledge the authenticity of objects of refuge. They advocate eternalism, naive rationalism, nihilism, or other false doctrines.* Wrong views can cause rebirth as an animal or as a human being of low acumen and little faith who lives without refuge or spiritual support.

One of the most discouraging outcomes of nonvirtue is its tendency toward repetition. For example, hell beings whose karma for having murdered has been exhausted to the point of their release from the torments of hell may be

---

*Eternalism holds that some entity—a material phenomenon, a state of being, or a divinity—has eternal existence, whereas naive rationalism finds validity in isolated events rather than embracing an all-encompassing view of reality. Nihilism holds that nothing exists and therefore nothing matters.

reborn in the human realm, but there they will become violent children—or children subjected to violence—who enjoy torturing pets, insects, and other children and who may murder again as adults. Nonvirtue creates an affinity for the unwholesome.

THE TEN VIRTUES

The ten virtuous actions are the opposite of the ten nonvirtuous ones: not killing, but instead protecting life; not stealing, but practicing generosity; not indulging in sexual misconduct, but practicing morality in sexual matters (enhanced by maintaining celibacy on certain sacred days and during certain times like spiritual retreats); not lying, but speaking the truth; not slandering, but speaking harmoniously; not speaking harshly, but using comforting words; not chattering, but speaking with discretion and meaning; not coveting, but rejoicing in the wealth and qualities of others; not bearing malice, but having goodwill; not holding wrong views, but cultivating right ones.

The karmic results are also the opposite of those of nonvirtue. We gain rebirth in the world of humans or gods with a pleasant and productive environment; we have long life and good health; we find wealth and resources; we have a good and loyal spouse or companion; we hear kind, gentle words of truth and praise; our own words are well spoken and well respected; we meet compatible friends; we get what we wish; helpers come to our assistance; we have natural acumen and easily comprehend the validity of spiritual doctrines.

Just as nonvirtuous actions foster a tendency toward repetition, so do virtuous actions. By practicing virtue, we develop an affinity for the wholesome that carries forward into future lifetimes.

MEDITATION INSTRUCTIONS

First, thoroughly assess your karmic situation. Survey the circumstances of this life to discern the karmic patterns established in the past, then check your current thoughts and actions as an indication of what will come. No sentient being in the six realms prefers suffering to happiness, yet almost all of us create the causes for misery. We act, oblivious to karmic consequences, seeking gratification in the moment, then blame our bad fortune on negative outer circumstances as if these represented random occurrences of fate rather than direct results of our own conduct.

Now, without equivocation, without hope of evading negative results if nonvirtue remains unpurified, bear honest witness to your own conduct. Others may praise you for your fine behavior, but only you truly know if your actions are tainted with impure motivation or poisonous emotions. Sooner or later you must journey through the after-death bardos, stripped of everything except consciousness and the forces of karma. Why sheathe yourself in hypocrisy and rationalizations now when you must stand naked then? Contemplate in this way, then rest the mind.

When thoughts arise, use them to arouse compassion. Imagine the karmic forces that overtake cruel aggressors when they die, the multiplicity of aggression that rebounds upon them, the aeons of torture in hell. Think of those whose comfortable lives are suddenly overwhelmed by tragedy, the unexpected consequence of unsuspected karma. Think of those whose lives remain comfortable and neutral, who extinguish possibilities for future well-being by using up the fruits of past good karma and not planting seeds for more. Contemplate lives almost devoid of opportunities to act with virtue—hell beings whose torment only infuriates them further, deprived spirits whose insatiable craving obsesses them, animals that are predatory by instinct. When the power of compassion motivates you to alleviate in any way possible all the sorrow arising from ignorance of karma, relax into uncontrived meditation.

When thoughts arise, direct them toward prayer. Pray that all beings may refine perfectly the sense of what to accept and what to reject. Pray that you may cease blaming others and begin purifying your own mind. Pray that through well-disciplined physical activity, well-chosen words, and beneficial intention, you may create the causes for fortunate circumstances. Pray that, ultimately, we may all escape this bewildering tangle of karma altogether and enter a state of pristine awareness. Then rest.

Finally, harnessing your thoughts once more, commit yourself to acting in accord with the most refined conduct and meditating until you establish the highest view. Then, again, rest.

SUFFERING

Not a single sentient being anywhere in the six realms abides in lasting happiness, and most experience misery almost beyond imagination. Now, as we rest in the relative peace and happiness of the human realm, we should reflect on suffering, to develop both deep renunciation of suffering's causes and profound compassion for all in its grip.

As with karma, we cannot attribute our suffering to some vengeful god or demon. The seeds of suffering germinate in our mind when the first slip into dualistic delusion evolves into self-centered attachment and aversion, which become the basis of flawed action and karmic consequences. In other words, our suffering arises from negative karma, which arises from nonvirtue, which in turn arises from nonrecognition of our own nondual nature. The dense projections that we label "the six realms" are part of a continuum that begins with dualistic confusion.

Suffering falls into three major categories—change, proliferation, and pervasiveness. These are the mechanisms of misery for all beings, from those in the highest, most blissful worldly god realms to those in the lowest hells.

The suffering of change is particularly intense in the human realm, because the mixture of karma that brings about rebirth here juxtaposes joy and sorrow. For example, we feel sunny, but a devastating telephone call—from our boss perhaps, or our stockbroker, doctor, or mother—changes our outlook entirely. We feel afflicted, not just by the bad news itself but also by the disintegration of the happiness we felt a moment before. Again and again the wearisome fluctuations of impermanence erode our pleasure and undercut our stability.

The proliferation of suffering, "suffering upon suffering," refers to one bad thing happening in tandem with another. We are embattled in a lawsuit and our love life falls apart; we are diagnosed as having a serious illness and we lose our job; a loved one dies and someone crashes into our car. At times it seems as if adversity comes from all directions and nothing is so bad that it cannot get worse. We wonder why bad events occur in clusters. Actually, every event stems from karma created in the past, and karmic results ripple through a life in their own time, just as if we had thrown a rock in a pond and now experience the waves. In fact, not a single rock but countless past karmic events create unpredictable, turbulent wave patterns in this life.

Pervasive suffering resembles the oil of a sesame seed, not apparent until we press the seed, or the dangerous undertow of a calm ocean, invisible until someone is pulled down. We, like most people, may often be comfortably oblivious to the suffering that saturates ordinary existence, that is inseparable from the web of conditioned existence. For example, most people eat without thought of the animals slaughtered for their meat, or the insects destroyed to grow their vegetables, or the toil and exposure to chemicals of the farmers and farm workers, or the greed involved in marketing. There are nonvirtue and suffering in every phase of bringing food to the table, despite the pleasure of eating. And so it is with every aspect of ordinary, comfortable existence. If we probe the surface, we discover pervasive, inescapable suffering.

Suffering reveals itself in the constant disturbances of the environment, in the negative interactions between beings, in the lack of freedom and enduring happiness. No one can sustain obliviousness indefinitely, because the very nature of samsara is suffering. We have an accumulation of negative karma and a store of mental poisons, so sooner or later the stresses of cyclic existence will bring suffering to the fore.

The teaching on the four thoughts usually includes graphic descriptions of suffering in the six realms. Nobody likes to imagine misery explicitly, particularly the horrors of hell. Tibetan dharma students, however, usually expect these teachings, whereas Western students are sometimes surprised and shocked when they are offered. Some think the lama is trying to indoctrinate by fear and do not come back.

Once, when Chagdud Rinpoche was giving extensive teachings on the realms, a woman who was tentatively exploring Buddhism came up to him after his presentation of the hells. "I'm a Catholic and I guess I'll stay Catholic," she said. "You Tibetan Buddhists have eighteen hells to deal with, while we have only one."

Certainly, to generate fear and exhaustion with samsaric suffering is one purpose of these teachings. Out of compassion, the teacher wishes to dispel students' ignorance of karmic consequences. However, a deeper motivation lies in arousing their compassion for all those trapped in the six realms and inspiring them to attain the power to lead these beings to liberation.

THE HELL REALM

As the most terrible of the three lower realms, hell is the ultimate reflection of delusion, the external projection of anger and hatred. Although no one can discover these regions by excavation or geographic search, the beings reborn there experience hell as intensely real, as real as our earth is to us. Layer upon dense layer of pain surrounds hell beings, suffusing them with pain, completely penetrating their consciousness. For this reason, they cannot generate a redeeming thought or action to purify their karma and must remain in hell interminably, until their karma exhausts itself of its own accord.

The eight hot hells are the projection of violent anger and rage, and are the karmic result of murder and other actions committed in anger. Beings there suffer horribly from torture and fire. In hell, beings do not have the luxury of death. Struck down by weapons, chopped into pieces, cudgeled, boiled, or burned, they revive and the torments repeat themselves in an endless nightmare.

The eight cold hells are the projection of icy, murderous hatred and hostility. Beings there freeze, until their frozen bodies crack open like fractured ice and they are eaten by creatures with flaming beaks. As in the hot hells, they do not die but remain bound in their frigid misery for many thousands of years.

Release from these hells does not lead directly into another realm, but into the near hells, nightmarish landscapes where plants with razor-sharp leaves slash at flesh, lakes transform into firepits, and friends appear, then metamorphose into demons.

Another kind of hell occurs when a bardo being enters an inanimate object, mistaking it for a womb. Thus, conscious beings are caught in trees, rocks, doorframes, and many other objects where they suffer as they are chopped, shattered, slammed, discarded, and so forth.

The sufferings of hell are terrible to envision and contemplate, yet if we deny hell, we subvert the benefit of our prayers and dedication of merit to the agonized beings there. Each of them has been our loving parent, and some may even be our deceased friends and relatives from this very lifetime. We may represent their only spiritual connection, the only one whose compassion they can rely on.

THE DEPRIVED SPIRIT REALM

Similarly, only by the prayers of practitioners and their offerings of food and drink can deprived spirits find a single particle of sustenance or a single moment of comfort. Their karma from craving, miserliness, paranoid obsession, and theft plays out as an utterly barren environment where they suffer all-consuming hunger and thirst. Their bodies mirror the distortions of their minds, burdening them with huge, distended bellies, spindly limbs, and tiny mouths like the eye of a needle that make it impossible to fill their cavernous bellies.

Some of these spirits, if they find ripe fruit, watch it immediately wither before their eyes, or if they reach clear water, see it evaporate. Others may find sustenance but are prevented by inner mental hindrances from partaking of it. Those who partake of food experience being burned from the inside out. Some see food and drink as revolting substances such as excrement, pus, and blood. Some cannibalize their own bodies. There are demons who, when in proximity to humans, inflict disease and mental illness. Though they may have the power to harm others, these spirits themselves suffer from their lack of substantiality, from paranoia and disquiet.

Spirits of yet another type live in great splendor similar to that of the worldly gods, but once every seven days they are tormented by experiences of death. Called "local deities" by Tibetans, they are named "spirit guides" by some Westerners who rely on them for psychic information. They are not reliable sources of knowledge or assistance, however, because, entrapped in their own cycles of vexation and pain, they are apt to mislead.

THE ANIMAL REALM

The animal realm, the third of the lower realms, reflects the karma of stupidity. The suffering of animals is obvious to us as human beings. They live as famished predators and fearful prey, beasts of burden and frustrated pets, livestock raised like crops for meat, and wildlife whose habitat has been polluted and destroyed. In our modern world, we increasingly inflict a special suffering on animals by imposing on them a completely unnatural environment. Whales of immense intelligence who normally journey through thousands of miles of the ocean are captured and placed in concrete pools. Gorillas, orangutans, and elephants are torn away from their family groups and their jungle homes, encaged, then gouged and beaten until they amuse us. Dogs, bred for centuries to live as companions to humans, are placed in medical laboratories and tortured, their vocal cords severed so technicians do not have to hear their pitiable cries.

Because animals have limited means of communicating with humans, we regard them with great callousness. Only by a great leap of imagination can we contemplate what it might be like if a completely alien but highly intelligent species came to dominate us—if with utter incomprehension of our human feelings they sorted us into breeding stocks, killed off the weak and old among us, as well as those who failed to meet specifications, forced us to reproduce and used us for meat and milk. These aliens might develop an affection for a certain type of us, bred and cared for—and easily abandoned—as pets. Some of us might be utilized in experiments, some trained to labor at alien tasks, some to perform. As humans, however, we would have no ability to tell our story, to express our feelings, in a way meaningful to our alien masters. They would determine our lives with complete disregard for our natural state of being.

Spiritually, the tragedy of animals lies in their having to endure what life brings them with little comprehension, little ability to elevate suffering into understanding or purification. Like other beings of the lower realms, animals can only wait until their torment exhausts itself through the playing out of their karma. Then, in the bardos that follow their death, the intelligence compressed into animal rebirth blazes forth momentarily and equals that of other bardo beings. If they have sufficiently purified previous karma, they find rebirth in the upper realms. If not, this intelligence is channeled into instinct and sensory responsiveness, and their consciousness enters either another animal birth or an even lower one if previously they have been vicious and greedy.

THE JEALOUS GOD REALM

The jealous god or titan realm, the karmic projection of virtue tainted by jealousy, resembles a magical kingdom with dazzling, jewel-studded palaces, fertile fields, and inhabitants who can perform awesome feats of mind and body. Yet in this realm, too, suffering prevails. Here, too, there is no lasting happiness, because the titans are prevented by their intense competitiveness, malice, and covetousness from enjoying their riches and extraordinary abilities. They quickly engage in strife and warfare with one another and with the pleasure-loving gods above them.

A wish-fulfilling tree is rooted in the jealous god realm, but the tree's fruit, filled with bliss-giving nectar, falls within the gods' realm above. The titans fixate on this perceived injustice and attack the gods. The gods arouse themselves from their indolent, sensual pleasures by drinking anger-provoking water from a monster's mouth and counterattack under the command of Indra, who rides the central head of a divine elephant with thirty-three heads, flanked by his ministers on the other thirty-two heads.

The gods are seven times larger than the jealous gods and cannot be mortally wounded except by decapitation. They recover from lesser wounds instantaneously by applying a healing elixir. The jealous gods, like humans, can be slain if struck at any vital point, and the weapons the gods unleash are far more powerful than those in the titans' arsenal. Kunkyong, the gods' crazed elephant, kills hundreds of thousands as he cuts through the ranks of the jealous gods with a wheel of swords spinning from his trunk.

Thus, the battle's outcome is predetermined and the fallen legions of titans slide down the side of Mount Meru, turning the great cosmic sea at the mountain's base red with their blood. Yet the jealous gods do not desist from their futile combat. Driven by their fierce delusions, they wage war again and again, and are defeated in terrible, never-ending cycles.

THE GOD REALM

The environment of the sensuous worldly gods, the karmic projection of mixed virtue and pride, is more magnificent and much more blissful than that of the titans. Worldly gods have no need to quarrel, because whatever they wish they can manifest through the power of mind. They live for hundreds or thousands of years, dallying in playful sport in an environment saturated with luxurious pleasure. It has been said that the finest silk of the human realm would look like a rag to a god; the most beautiful woman, a shriveled crone; the most brilliant jewel, a worthless bauble.

Above the sensuous gods, the gods of the form and formless meditational levels have no need of substance for pleasure. For them bliss and tranquillity arise from substanceless states of mind. They live longer than the sensuous gods, sometimes for aeons.

Yet, as long-lived as the gods are, they do not live forever, and their death is a source of immense suffering. For the formless gods, who have no corporeal bodies, death means a descent from a sublime state of mind to a grosser one and entrapment by corporeality. The first sign of this impending fall presents itself as a thought or fixation, an irritating distraction from pure absorption. Gradually, knowing what is happening but powerless to prevent it, the gods are pulled deeper and deeper into the treacherous currents of distraction and toward the mind states of lower sentient beings.

For the sensuous gods, fading flower garlands and garments turning soiled and tattered mark the first signs of death's approach. The gods, delightfully fragrant before, begin to perspire and their bodies eventually reek. They become discontented with their thrones. Their companions, sensing that death is approaching, escort them to distant gardens. There, having offered farewell wishes that they find rebirth in the human realm, these companions forsake them to continue their own carefree lives uninterrupted.

Alone, conscious through clairvoyant power of the lower destination that awaits them, the gods languish grief-stricken on the threshold of death for three hundred and fifty human years. The blissful fruit of their previous virtue has dried up unreplenished, and their pride and self-centered oblivion have isolated them. In this barren, parched state of mind, a landscape of wasted opportunities, they die. The most fortunate find rebirth in the human realm; most fall lower because of the anger that arises as they pass through the bardo.

THE HUMAN REALM

The human realm represents a mixture of karma, of virtue combined with the five poisons. Since a single poison does not predominate as it does in the other five realms, the human realm offers a perceptual fluidity unknown elsewhere. Whereas a hell being experiences nonstop torture for an aeon and a formless god experiences blissful absorption for an equally long time, we humans can experience torment and bliss in one day. A person in black despair over a relationship, for example, might suddenly find reconciliation and the heights of happiness. Certainly such despair does not equal the torture of hell and such happiness does not equal the gods' bliss, but the sweeping movements of humans through different mental states are unparalleled in other realms. Humans therefore experience both the suffering of change and the potential of change.

Birth, old age, sickness, and death create inherent suffering for human beings. As well, the secondary miseries of separation from loved ones, encountering aggravating and hostile people, not fulfilling desires, and meeting undesirable circumstances bring about tremendous unhappiness.

Regarding birth, in the West we find accurate physiological descriptions of the stages of gestation, but these do not mention what the consciousness of the unborn being experiences throughout the process. Tibetan teachings clearly describe the experiences of the consciousness before birth.

After death, if beings are not fortunate enough to find liberation in the bardo of the true nature of reality, they enter the bardo of becoming. There the five aggregates—form, feeling, evaluation, volition, and consciousness—become coarser and a mental body develops. This mental body, amid a great turmoil of hallucinations and noise, begins to long for a corporeal body as a means to escape being blown about helplessly by the winds of karma. Exactly according to its karma, the bardo being moves toward its destined rebirth.

If this rebirth is to be in the human realm, the bardo being will be drawn toward a couple in the act of intercourse, and the karmic winds will force the consciousness into the union of sperm and egg. At this point the suffering of birth begins. The unborn child, thus encapsulated, must endure nine months in the dark, foul restriction of the womb. Heat, cold, the motions of its mother, the ill-effects of what she eats all torment the unborn child, although in no way as much as the passage of birth itself, the forced transit through a narrow channel into the harsh air and glaring light of the world. The newborn child can only wail in its misery.

The distress of old age goes far beyond its well-known physical infirmities, though these are very hard to bear. Perhaps worse are our lack of enjoyments, loss of interest, loneliness. Many of our friends have already died or are inaccessible in hospitals and nursing homes. Communicating with others becomes difficult, because our sight and hearing fail. In any case, few seek conversation with people who are old, ugly, and outside of life's mainstream, however respected they once were. We become increasingly isolated and our memory fails. In the growing confusion, fear of death overwhelms us. Like children, we are easily upset and no one can offer sufficient comfort. The collapse of dignity is humiliating. With no will to live yet dreading death, we witness our vitality slowly ebb away.

Sickness, like old age, brings physical pain, confusion, and unhappiness, all hard to bear. Many people cannot find or afford the treatment they need, and even those who find treatment often encounter much frustration. Just when we feel most fragile and unable to cope, troublesome and expensive decisions must be made. Advice comes from all directions, but who can enter our situation and really understand it? We feel alienated, exhausted, dazed, and suffocated by pain and problems. Other areas of life begin to unravel and we are helpless to prevent such loss. If we are self-reliant, dependency on others is humiliating and irritating. If we have adjusted to dependency, it is still hard to escape listlessness and boredom. We wonder, wouldn't it be easier to die?

When death actually approaches, however, it brings a magnitude of suffering far greater than that of old age or sickness. We may have thought we had nothing to live for, but the final severance from friends, family, possessions, all the events of our life, and, most of all, the parting from our own cherished body create unsurpassed anguish. The physical changes as we near death frighten us: the senses fail and the mind becomes disoriented. Utterly alone, we must deal with the transition of dying with whatever resources we have left. As physical and mental strength dwindles, spiritual attainment is the only such resource of real value. If our attainment is meager, after death we will pass through the bardo of the true nature of reality without recognizing our own absolute nature and we will endure the bardo of rebirth without spiritual refuge. No one should underestimate the suffering of death.

But sickness and death are far from the sole sources of human pain. Separation from loved ones, whether by life's circumstances or by death, brings pain so sharp we feel we've been stabbed in the heart. We may awaken in the middle of the night, disconsolate and lonely, with no power to reverse what has happened and no hope of regaining former joys. Like water from a deep and bitter well, tears flow from a source of grief so profound it is almost unbearable.

Further, encountering undesirable people brings unpleasantness, loss, anxiety, and sometimes outright life-threatening harm. At unpredictable times we may meet a surly stranger, a quarrelsome acquaintance, or a crazy enemy, someone with whom we have an unknown karmic connection who tries to kill us for no apparent reason. Or in the place where we live or work we become caught up with people with degraded values and cannot extricate ourselves. The possibilities proliferate. Again and again negative people turn up, in both abrupt confrontations and sustained relationships, causing untold losses of property, well-being, and peace.

The frustration of not getting what we want, not achieving worldly goals, and not finding the happiness we seek sours life. We become resigned to disappointment after disappointment. An insidious resentment begins to poison our perspective, making it even harder to succeed and diminishing the pleasure of accomplishment.

The frustration of not getting what we want equals the difficulty of holding what we have. Thieves steal our possessions, slanderers undercut our reputation, ambitious competitors menace our position. Besieged in this way, we find little pleasure in what we have acquired. Even as abundance increases, we feel more and more like a deprived spirit.

MEDITATION INSTRUCTIONS

Begin by contemplating suffering, focusing on the six realms. Vividly imagine existence within each one. Your mind can enter other realms through the power of visualization, which allows them to unfold in your experience. The potential for any experience abides in the mind. In contemplation, extrapolate from a moment of pain you have actually felt—scalding water, perhaps, or biting winter winds numbing your toes and fingertips—to the extreme, all-encompassing pain of the hot or cold hells. Moments of hunger and thirst magnify into the famished, parched deprivation of the spirit realm. So your mind can journey.

If the experiences of other realms lie too far outside the scope of your imagination, contemplation of human suffering is enough. For example, put yourself in the place of someone caught in a war zone, in constant fear of being maimed or killed, surrounded by devastation, separated from friends and family, confronted by brutal inhumanity and hatred. Even to rejoice in violent victory over enemies creates terrible karma. How much more tragic the forced participation in the killing! No one is exempt from the downward spiral— not the leaders who will be karmically accountable for every injury and death that occurs because of their orders; not the soldiers who carry out the killing; not the victims who are catapulted into the bardo with their minds inflamed with anger.

This human realm has no scarcity of suffering. The depth of your contemplation depends on really placing yourself inside such situations and allowing yourself to feel what others have felt, to stand in their shoes. When this has been accomplished and the mind yearns for cessation, drop all thoughts and rest.

When thoughts intervene, generate compassion. Think of the countless beings in the six realms. In the course of innumerable rebirths, each of them has been your parent. They are caught in cycles of misery and have no idea how to extricate themselves. Think of their predicament until compassion wells up as the wish that their present suffering be alleviated immediately and that ultimately they be liberated from the sorrows of samsara altogether. Then, again, drop all thoughts and rest.

When thoughts flood into your meditation, direct them toward prayer. Pray that suffering not sweep you away and that you see whatever arises as purification. In the confusion that suffering brings, pray not to create karmic causes for more misery. Pray as well that you attain the power to lead others from the depths of samsara to a state beyond sorrow.

Pray that all beings be liberated from the endless cycles of samsaric suffering. Relax in uncontrived meditation. When thoughts arise once more, make a firm commitment to practice the path until you attain liberation from suffering, for the sake of all beings. Before, as you yourself were drowning in the ocean of samsara, you could not rescue others. Now, by the skillful means of the path, there is hope of escape. Resolve not to sink back, not to abandon others, and then rest in the peace of natural relaxation.

THE EXTRAORDINARY
PRELIMINARIES

REFUGE

Once we have considered the causes and conditions of cyclic existence in the context of the four thoughts, the need to find release from this turbulent ocean of suffering becomes urgent. We long to go beyond relative reality to absolute truth. The impure experience explored through the outer preliminaries gives way to pure experience revealed through the extraordinary preliminaries of refuge and bodhicitta, mandala offerings, Vajrasattva purification, guru yoga, and transference of consciousness.

Each of these practices sets the stage for realization of the absolute nature of all appearances. Visualizations of Guru Rinpoche, Vajrasattva, and Amitabha engage the pure form aspect of the lama, and recitation of prayers and mantra the lama's pure speech. Meditative concentration and resting nondually in the absolute lama call forth the lama's enlightened mind. Our faith in the lama at the outset of the extraordinary preliminary practices is consummated by the nondual experience of the three secret vajras, that is, the experience of all form, sound, and mental events as inseparable from the vajra (enlightened) body, speech, and mind of the lama.

Seeking protection from samsara, seeking enlightenment, we find refuge in the Three Jewels of the Buddhadharma—

in the Buddha Shakyamuni, who flawlessly demonstrated the path to enlightenment; in the dharma, his teachings; and in the sangha, those who follow the path he demonstrated and hold unbroken lineage transmission. In Vajrayana, other names for the sources of refuge are the "Three Roots" and "Three Kayas." Through ngondro practice and the teachings of our lama, we come to view the sources of refuge—the Three Jewels, Roots, and Kayas—not as nine entities, but as nine facets of absolute refuge, interdependent and inseparable.

As Vajrayana practitioners, we take refuge from now until enlightenment with the bodhicitta motivation to lead all beings to liberation. In the context of the *Dudjom Tersar Ngondro*, we recite prayers of refuge and bodhicitta together as we perform prostrations. In other ngondros, practitioners recite refuge only during prostrations, and bodhicitta is completed afterward, as a separate practice. However, in the oral instructions given by His Holiness Dudjom Jigdral Yeshe Dorje for the *Tersar Ngondro*, both prayers are recited. Bodhicitta exalts our sense of refuge. We understand that all beings are ensnared in the predicament of samsara. When we pray for protection, we pray that they likewise will find safety and refuge. When we pray for enlightenment, we pray that we can guide them to that same state. We include all beings in every prostration through visualization, prayer, and intention.

THE THREE JEWELS: BUDDHA, DHARMA, SANGHA

Buddha refers to the Buddha Shakyamuni, the fourth of a thousand buddhas who will appear in this age. An emanation of the nirmanakaya buddha of Ogmin pureland, he was born as a prince of the Shakya clan in India and enjoyed the pleasures of royalty. When confronted with the suffering of the human condition, he renounced his worldly birthright and practiced austerities for six years. Even strenuous austerities did not bring about the realization he sought, however, so he sat down under a bodhi tree in Bodhgaya, India, and vowed not to leave until he had attained complete enlightenment.

The forces of Mara tried to overwhelm him with their manifestations of delusion, first by seduction, then by attack, but they failed to deflect him from his attainment of absolute truth. When he stood up, he had reached full enlightenment. He then turned the wheel of dharma three times for the benefit of sentient beings and taught the path of dharma. Eventually the supreme good fortune of beings to have him present on this earth exhausted itself. He then passed beyond our world of suffering into parinirvana.

The Tibetan word for buddha is *sang-gye*. *Sang* means that all faults, obscurations, and defilements have dissolved; *gye* means that all qualities of wisdom are complete. By this definition countless beings have reached enlightenment and become buddhas. The Buddha's example demonstrated the accomplishment of both these aspects of enlightenment. He ceased doing any nonvirtue and practiced virtue thoroughly. Over countless lifetimes he showed the path of selfless compassion, even giving the flesh of his own body to benefit another. In his final lifetime on this earth, he accomplished twelve significant deeds, as do all buddhas, that revealed him as a buddha. He left Ogmin for this world in the form of an ash-white elephant; entered the womb of his mother, Maya Devi; took birth in Lumbini, then took seven steps in each of the four directions; learned the arts such as writing, mathematics, and archery; engaged in sports with other young men and enjoyed the company of his consorts; abandoned the princely life at the age of twenty-nine to become a self-ordained monk; endured hardships for six years; sat beneath the bodhi tree in Bodhgaya; defeated hosts of demons the night before his enlightenment; attained buddhahood at dawn; turned the wheel of dharma at Sarnath, India; and passed into parinirvana.

Upon his enlightenment, the Buddha Shakyamuni demonstrated the thirty-two major and eighty minor marks of enlightened body—he was perfectly proportioned, his feet did not touch the ground, he had a spherical protrusion on the top of his head, he was surrounded by a nimbus of light, and so forth. Likewise, he attained the sixty signs of enlightened speech—he could project his voice to any distance and to all realms without raising it, his words were understood in various languages and at different levels of meaning simultaneously, he spoke in a manner melodious, pleasant, and always exactly appropriate to each being's needs, and so forth.

The Buddha's enlightened qualities of mind yielded omniscient understanding of the causes and conditions of all phenomena, both in their manifest appearance and in their ultimate, empty essence. He knew each being's thoughts and had unobstructed knowledge of past, present, and future. So it is that when we take refuge in the Buddha, we accept the support of an infallible guide, flawless, replete with all qualities of enlightenment.

The Buddha taught eighty-four thousand methods in three turnings of the wheel of dharma to benefit sentient beings and enable them to reach a state of enlightenment no different from his own. His teachings comprise the dharma, the second of the Three Jewels. His first turning of the wheel took place in the Deer Park in Sarnath, where he taught the four noble truths: the truth of suffering, the truth of the cause of suffering, the truth of the cessation of suffering, and the truth of the path to the cessation of suffering. The second turning of the wheel occurred at Vulture's Peak in

Rajgir when the Buddha taught the *Prajna Paramita*, the "Perfection of Wisdom." The third turning consisted of the "Doctrine of Absolute Truth," which he taught to extraordinary beings such as bodhisattvas, gods, nagas, rakshas, and humans. The second and third turnings of the wheel encompass the entire Mahayana path.

The scriptures of the Buddha's teachings were collected into the Tripitaka, or "Three Baskets"—the vinaya, which deals with lay and monastic discipline; the sutras, which are the actual discourses of the Buddha; and the abhidharma, which details the formation, structure, and processes of the universe and sentient beings, and which delineates the levels on the path to enlightenment. The scriptures also include the shastras, or commentaries, and the tantras, specifically the Vajrayana transmission.

According to tradition, the tantras were first opened to King Indrabodhi. One day the king was standing on the balcony of his palace when he saw the Buddha flying through the air with his retinue of arhats. King Indrabodhi asked his minister who these extraordinary beings were and whether they might accept an invitation to the midday meal at his palace.

So the king offered the Buddha a fine meal, and the Buddha in turn gave him a teaching on renunciation of worldly attachment. The king listened attentively, but at the conclusion inquired if the Buddha could offer a teaching that did not require renouncing his duties as a sovereign, his pleasures, or his wealth. "I am a king," he said, "and hundreds of thousands of my subjects depend on me. I cannot abandon my responsibilities."

The Buddha in his omniscience recognized that King Indrabodhi had the karma to practice Vajrayana, and at a later time opened the Guhyasamaja mandala to him by appearing in the sky as deity and retinue and by bestowing empowerment and teachings. The king practiced so well that not only he but his subjects reached enlightenment.

In his lifetime the Buddha Shakyamuni prophesied that he would emanate in the future to continue the Vajrayana teachings, and specifically that he would be born in a lotus. This prophecy was fulfilled by the lotus birth of Guru Rinpoche, in Orgyan in the eighth century.

After the Buddha's passing into parinirvana, the Vajrayana teachings were transmitted through Vajrapani and the eighty-four mahasiddhas, who held not only the lineages of scriptural and oral transmission, but also certain esoteric lineages. The Nyingma tradition of Vajrayana Buddhism classifies the entire Buddhist path into nine vehicles (Skt. *yanas*)— the three causal vehicles of the sravaka, the pratyekabuddha, and the bodhisattva, and the six resultant vehicles, which include the outer tantras of kriya, upa, and yoga, and the inner tantras of maha, anu, and ati.

In the Nyingma tradition, the dharma is transmitted through the long lineage of oral transmissions (*kama*) and as *termas*, or "treasures," concealed by Guru Rinpoche and his consort Yeshe Tsogyal, to be revealed at a later time to meet the exact needs of practitioners. These termas can be classified as earth termas (*sa ter*), which involve physical objects, and mind termas (*gong ter*), which are discovered in the mindstream of a treasure revealer (*terton*). These termas, like a fire rekindled, are then reestablished as mainstream lineage transmissions. Thus, the jewel of dharma represents refuge in all of the Buddha's teachings—the scriptures, the direct oral transmissions, and the various esoteric lineage transmissions. Indeed, like facets of a wish-fulfilling gem, these overflow with the bounty of realization.

Sangha includes all who have taken refuge in the Buddhadharma. In Tibetan *gedun* is the word for sangha. *Ge* means "virtue," *dun* means "to yearn for"—thus, the sangha

consists of those who strive to practice virtue. At the Hinayana level the term "sangha" refers to sravakas and pratye-
kabuddhas; at the Mahayana level it refers to bodhisattvas,
the spiritual sons and daughters of the Buddha. Buddhists
practicing any level of the path are esteemed as sangha and
as spiritual companions. However, only bodhisattvas of the
highest order actually form an infallible refuge.

Those of the Mahayana sangha survey the misery of samsara, and feel compassion and desire to help others who share
this predicament. According to the commentaries, even before they take refuge, some signs of their affinity to the Mahayana path appear, the most important being a kind heart,
concern for others, a wholesome character, and a natural
mindfulness. Many Western practitioners look back with
some dismay at their lives before they entered Buddhism,
but certainly these underlying Mahayana qualities were present and became readily enhanced by the training of the
bodhisattva path.

Mahayana Buddhists take refuge with the extensive motivation to accomplish enlightenment through selfless effort on
behalf of others. With this altruistic intention they engage in
bodhisattva training until the two veils—afflictive emotions
and intellectual obscurations—are removed. At that point,
they attain flawless recognition of their own absolute nature,
which allows the pure qualities of mind to arise naturally,
without obstruction. The bodhisattva, with a final vow to benefit sentient beings according to their specific needs, becomes
a buddha whose compassion radiates like a thousand suns
and who continually sends forth emanations to benefit beings.

THE THREE ROOTS: LAMA, YIDAM, KHADRO

In Tibetan *la* means that which is "highest and most
precious"; *ma* means "mother." Just as a mother expresses

love and compassion for her children, so the lama shows unsurpassed love and compassion for sentient beings. The lama remains inseparable from the Buddha, but for Vajrayana practitioners, the lama's kindness is even greater and more direct than the Buddha's because the lama has taken rebirth to teach and guide them. The lama embodies the source of all blessing through empowerments, teachings, and lineage transmission, including the mind-to-mind transmission of Great Perfection.

Yidam means the bond established through pure Vajrayana commitment (Skt. *samaya;* Tib. *damtsig*). The yidam is the chosen meditational deity, the deity with whom the practitioner has an abiding bond. Accomplishing the deity's meditation brings forth in the practitioner the qualities of the deity. These qualities, inseparable from mind's absolute nature, have always been the practitioner's own qualities, but like gold in unrefined ore they remain hidden. Meditating on the yidam refines away obscurations. The yidam serves as the source of all siddhis, the extraordinary spiritual accomplishments that benefit others.

Khadro is the Tibetan term for the Sanskrit *dakini; kha* means "sky" or "space" in the sense of dharmadhatu, and *dro* means "goer." The khadro goes without obstruction through space, fulfilling the lama's enlightened activity. Embodying the female principle of pristine awareness (*yeshey*), dakinis manifest at various levels, including that of humans; the great practitioners Yeshe Tsogyal and Machig Labdron, for example, were dakinis.

THE THREE KAYAS:
DHARMAKAYA, SAMBHOGAKAYA, NIRMANAKAYA

Dharmakaya is the absolute nature of being, empty yet replete with all qualities, completely pervasive yet not obvious to ordinary perception. Dharmakaya is mind's absolute nature, beyond concepts and mental fabrications. In the context of our own mindstream, dharmakaya is *rigpa,* intrinsic awareness; in the context of mind itself, suchness, dharmakaya is *yeshey,* pristine awareness. In Tibetan, dharmakaya is *chhö ku, chhö* meaning "all phenomena," *ku* meaning "body." The nature of all phenomena, all that appears, is dharmakaya—original purity, devoid of characteristics, devoid of color, shape, form, coming, going, or dwelling. Like space, which contains the whole spectrum of phenomena, from the most momentary energy of a subatomic particle to the enduring manifestation of suns and planets, dharmakaya is the source of all—mother dharmakaya. Dharmakaya as the foundation of the display of all phenomena corresponds to a clear crystal.

Sambhogakaya is the pure, spontaneous, unceasing display of dharmakaya. In Tibetan, sambhogakaya is *longkyod dzogpai ku, long* meaning "wealth," *kyod* meaning "enjoy," *dzog* meaning "complete," *pai* being a connecting word, and *ku* meaning "body." The rich yet subtle display of the sambhogakaya is fully enjoyed as the limitless wealth of pure perceptions by tenth-level bodhisattvas, who have removed all afflictive emotions and have only extremely subtle intellectual obscurations that cast a veil between them and enlightenment. Ordinary beings cannot see it. Vajrayana practitioners visualize deities in sambhogakaya form, but it is not until their practice becomes very deep and pure that the sambhogakaya display reveals itself spontaneously in their minds. In meditation, sambhogakaya is experienced as the lucidity, the spontaneous energy, that arises from mind's dharmakaya aspects of intrinsic awareness and emptiness. The sambhogakaya corresponds to the potentiality of rainbow light radiance within a crystal, the energy that gives rise to the display.

Nirmanakaya is the emanation body that arises from the unobstructed compassion of enlightened ones to benefit sentient beings. In Tibetan, nirmanakaya is *trul ku, trul* meaning "emanation," *ku* meaning "body." Because the dharmakaya and sambhogakaya remain obscured to ordinary perception, the nirmanakaya manifests the denser appearances that sentient beings can perceive through their sense faculties and their minds' concepts. In the impure perception of ordinary beings, nirmanakaya is experienced as the afflictive emotions and intellectual obscurations of samsara. In the pure perception of a meditator, nirmanakaya is experienced as the inseparability of emptiness and lucidity emanating as non-referential responsiveness to the needs of sentient beings wherever and however they arise. The nirmanakaya thus arises like the rainbows that emanate from a crystal.

PRECEPTS OF REFUGE

Refuge in the Three Jewels may be limited to one vow—not to kill—or the precepts may be delineated as five, or as nine. The nine are closely interrelated.

The three things to abandon:
• Harming others
• Taking refuge in those who are not infallible wisdom beings
• Holding as friends and influential associates persons who are extremely nonvirtuous

The three things to do:
• Respect the form of the Buddha, as in statues and other images
• Respect the dharma, especially dharma texts
• Respect the sangha, especially the monastic sangha

Three additional precepts:
• Hold your lama as the jewel of the Buddha
• Hold your lama's words as the jewel of the dharma
• Hold your lama's retinue as the jewel of the sangha

The single most important vow is not to harm, and particularly not to kill, other beings. Harming others violates our own spiritual being. It is impossible to venerate and hold to the wisdom of the Three Jewels on one hand and to inflict harm on the other. By the very nature of enlightened intention, the Three Jewels offer protection and alleviation of suffering to sentient beings. When, as a member of the sangha, we follow the Buddha's example and teachings, it should become unthinkable for us to cause harm deliberately by hurting others or taking their lives. We should also develop great mindfulness about not causing harm through carelessness. It is not always possible to avoid stepping on ants, for example, but we should try. The reflexes of an undistracted and compassionate mind become very quick.

"Those who are not infallible wisdom beings" refers especially to teachers who do not have full qualities, to the worldly gods that Tibetans call "local deities," and to the deities of false religions. The qualities of a lama have been described in the chapter on the invocation, and local deities have been described in the section on the deprived spirit realm. These local deities are not wisdom beings even though their prophecies and occasional direct intervention on behalf of humans may sometimes seem to be a manifestation of wisdom. We should be very careful not to rely on them or on the psychics and oracles who channel them. Many people have been led down mistaken paths, and some into extremely black regions of mental confusion, by holding false gods infallible. Religions that require animal sacrifices or holy wars or similar nonvirtuous acts seem the very antithesis of wisdom.

Close association with extremely nonvirtuous people is detrimental, particularly at the beginning of our spiritual journey, when the path depends greatly on the pure companionship of friends and teachers. Just as a vine entwined around a sandalwood tree takes on the perfume of the sandalwood oil, so grass growing in a swamp is permeated by the stench of the muck. Thus, until we have thoroughly integrated dharma training into our mindstream, we should protect our practice by pure companionship.

Statues and pictorial images of the Buddha express the Buddha's enlightened intention that the seed of liberation be planted in the mindstream of whoever sees his form, even an artistic representation. Our reverence makes us receptive to this blessing, so we should never criticize the aesthetics of statues or paintings unless we are in a position to correct them, and we should never step over a statue or handle even a fragment of it carelessly.

The dharma is the blessing of the Buddha's enlightened intention that the seed of liberation be planted in the mindstream of whoever hears his words. For this reason we place Buddhist texts on a high shelf and not on the floor. We never step over them, and when we must dispose of papers that have even one word of dharma meaning—even an address with our dharma name—we should find a way to burn them rather than throw them into the trash. Tibetans hold a single letter of the alphabet as sacred and burn every paper with any kind of writing. Though this is perhaps impractical here in the West, still we must be aware of the sacred potential of written words and treat them with respect.

In discussing the dharma we must never provoke others into nonvirtuous, anti-Buddhist reactions and activities, because of the negative karma they will then incur. We, too, will incur negative karma if we impede others' entrance into the dharma or misdirect them on the path by unskillful or sectarian talk about spiritual issues.

Showing respect for the sangha begins with deference to those who wear monastic robes. The ordination of monks and nuns indicates their acceptance of the Buddha's rules of discipline. Tremendous virtue accrues from this. Although we may observe a humorous camaraderie among a group of monks, for our part it is inappropriate to speak roughly or teasingly to them. And just as we should never step over a text, we should never step over a monastic robe.

If we hold the precept to venerate our teacher as the Buddha, would we show him or her less than the utmost respect? Would we serve our lama with less than the limits of our ability? Would we offer only a meager portion of our resources and even begrudge him or her the offerings of others? If the Buddha walked into the room, would we remain seated? If the Buddha wished to eat, would we serve him haphazardly, with less than the best food? Would we mistrust the Buddha, look for flaws to justify our own scant faith? Would we contradict the Buddha's enlightened intention by insisting on our own way?

Maintaining this precept, we naturally develop pure perception of our lama as the Buddha, as the manifestation of the Buddha's enlightened mind. We conduct ourselves in a way that honors his or her kindness. We increase our receptivity to the flow of blessings from our teacher and begin to see everything as the lama's sacred manifestation. This holds true not only for positive, pleasurable appearances, but also for such difficulties as sickness, hostile attacks, and hardships. When negativity arises, we rely more deeply on our teacher, not just to alleviate bad outer circumstances, but to guide us in the application of spiritual methods. In the end, by our teacher's supreme blessing and enlightened intention, we transcend both hope and fear and free ourselves from the outer and inner limitations imposed by such duality.

Holding the lama's speech as the jewel of the dharma means that we listen with reverence and try to follow its subtle direction without disobeying a single point. We cultivate the pure perception that these words are the Buddha's words and convey transcendent wisdom undiminished over centuries. If we maintain this view, everything the lama says becomes a teaching, timeless and immediate. Sound itself becomes the lama's speech.

Holding the lama's retinue as the jewel of the sangha means that we perceive it purely as the physical manifestation of the lama's body. Ultimately, the sangha represents the nondual expression of the lama's enlightened form, and we perceive those in the sangha as extraordinary beings— dharma protectors, dakas, and dakinis. Just as we see the lama as the Buddha's mind and the lama's speech as the Buddha's teaching, we see the sangha as the Buddha's body.

In Vajrayana we understand that the connection with our lama has been established over many lifetimes, and likewise so has the connection with our lama's students. We respect and regard them as our spiritual companions. Certainly in a Vajrayana mandala, we must appreciate that these are in no way ordinary beings. We consider how rare it is to meet anyone in the six realms who follows the Buddha's example, how rarer still to meet those who seek enlightenment in order to liberate others, and how truly extraordinary to meet a Vajrayana practitioner who aspires to recognize mind's absolute nature.

If negativity about members of the sangha creeps into our mind, we should not act on it or try to rationalize it in any ordinary way. Particularly, we should not talk divisively. This is an easy mistake to make and it immediately sullies the purity of our path. Instead of finding fault outwardly, we should look back at our own mind and see the corresponding fault there. If our own mind were flawless, it would perceive only the essential purity of whatever arises. Since it is flawed by afflictive emotions and intellectual obscurations, it perceives impurities. Knowing this, we should use the dharma as a mirror to discover the imperfections of our own mind and eliminate them.

This is not commonsense advice—others have faults and of course we can observe them. Should we blind ourselves to the obvious? Yet we have habitually observed, judged, analyzed, and criticized others for quite a while, and this has not fulfilled our spiritual aspirations. To the contrary, such actions make denser the layers of concepts we are trying to clear away. We would be wiser to work with our own mind and simply pray that our sangha companions find whatever guidance they need to perfect their paths.

By taking refuge continuously, we develop irrevocable faith, and the flow of blessings—especially of protection and progress on the spiritual path—likewise becomes irreversible. Here in the West, we are very fortunate not to be confronted with life-and-death decisions about practicing the religion of our choice. In Tibet this was not so after the Chinese Communist takeover. However, even in terrible times of persecution, most Tibetans sustained inner faith in the Three Jewels. We do not need to say anything aloud or show anything outwardly in order to practice. If we carry our practice in our heart and display it only at appropriate moments and to sympathetic people, we will avoid many conflicts. This is important not only for our well-being. Remembering the wisdom qualities of the Three Jewels again and again uplifts our mind to its highest aspirations and guides our conduct on the path.

BODHICITTA

THE FOUR IMMEASURABLES: WISHING BODHICITTA

Compassion, equanimity, love, and joy—these are the four qualities of wishing bodhicitta, the aspiration to benefit all beings by attaining enlightenment. These qualities act as catalysts of spiritual development, dissolving self-centeredness and creating a sense of connectedness with all sentient beings. Through meditation we may experience them nondually as the qualities of absolute bodhicitta, arising unobstructed within the realization of emptiness, immeasurable.

To cultivate these four qualities, we move through stages of reflection, prayer, and commitment, allowing the mind to rest in nonconceptual meditation after each stage. We begin with compassion, the wish that others not suffer. We think of our own parents first, and of the suffering cyclic existence will inevitably bring them. We find their pain and sorrow distressing—as if we were on the shore of a turbulent ocean, watching them haplessly drift and struggle until they drowned. Certainly we would not ignore them, nor would we abandon the countless others who have been our kind parents in past lifetimes. From the depths of our hearts we long for their deliverance.

As the suffering of others becomes unbearable to us, we extend our compassion to one being after another until all are completely permeated with it. Compassion becomes nonreferential, the spontaneous reflex of our being. We are continuously motivated by the wish to alleviate sentient beings' pain in the moment and ultimately to lead them to a state beyond sorrow.

We reflect in this way, then drop all thoughts and rest the mind in nonconceptual meditation. When thoughts stir, we pray to the enlightened ones that they direct their power and wisdom so that we, too, will attain the enlightened capacity to alleviate the suffering of all beings, to liberate them from the pit of samsara. Then we rest. Finally, we make the commitment to live according to the most compassionate expression of our buddha nature. Again, we rest.

Next we cultivate equanimity, first by thinking of our countless rebirths and our connection with every being. At times each one—including those who are now strangers, unpleasant acquaintances, or outright enemies—has been our parent and has shown us great kindness. The wheel of samsara revolves endlessly: enemies become allies and allies become antagonists; close relatives are reborn in distant realms and from distant realms come our children. The nature of our relationship with any individual constantly shifts. Because nothing remains fixed or guaranteed, holding some close and keeping others at a distance feels troubling, narrow, distorted, and unbalanced.

Then we think about the fundamental sameness of sentient beings—at the most basic level, their buddha nature and, beyond that, their universal wish for happiness. In these respects, all are equal to one another and to us. Knowing this causes false distinctions to dissolve and a deep-seated peace and impartiality toward all beings to emerge. Our understanding that all have shown us the kindness of our own mother exalts them in equality.

Having reached this point in our cultivation of equanimity, we relax into uncontrived meditation. When thoughts flood into this moment, we pray to overcome the long-established habit of judging, of placing some high, some low, of helping some and harming others. We pray to develop the calm open-mindedness and impartiality of equanimity. Then we rest. Finally, we mentally state our commitment to overcome habitual judgment, habitual clinging to some and indifference to others, and to act with equal regard, love, and compassion for all beings. Once more, we rest.

To cultivate love, we think of the person we most treasure and allow a strong, genuine wish for this person's happiness to surge forth. The selfless desire that another find happiness—both the temporary happiness of favorable conditions within samsara and the ultimate happiness of enlightenment—is the Buddhist definition of love. Since happiness stems from virtue, love consists of a wish for virtue and the positive circumstances it creates. Like the devotion a great-hearted mother has for her only child, our love should be both unconditional and coupled with the desire that beings have a wholesome character to ensure happiness.

After we have established our loving wish for the happiness of our dearest ones, we extend it undiluted to one being after another, until we have touched every being throughout the reaches of space. Even our heartbeat resounds with the aspiration "May we all find happiness, may you, and you . . ."

Having expanded our love mentally, we relax the mind, resting until thoughts stir. Then we pray to the victorious ones that we will gain the capacity to enhance the happiness of all beings, to bring forth in them the unchangeable happiness of realization. Again, the mind relaxes. Finally, we commit ourselves to a path of loving kindness that excludes no one, has no limitations, and we conclude with relaxation into meditation beyond concept.

We accomplish the fourth immeasurable quality, that of joy, by rejoicing in the happiness of others, by looking for sparks of happiness and kindling them with our prayers and good intention. If we see someone enjoying a moment of affection, the warmth of a sunny day, some delicious food— any happy event, however small—we make the wish that they will never lose this measure of joy and that by their virtue it will only increase. For those whose lives are filled with pleasures, we rejoice without envy or reservation, recognizing that this represents the fruit of their past virtue. A joyous outlook brings a total lack of envy and a natural calmness.

We cultivate joy in this way, then relax the mind in nonconceptual meditation until thoughts arouse us to prayer: "May the virtue and happiness of each being increase continuously until at last all find the unchanging happiness of enlightenment." This aspiration carries us into the next phase of uncontrived rest, which is followed by the commitment to rejoice in and enhance whatever well-being we encounter. We conclude by resting in natural, uncontrived ease.

When we consciously cultivate these four qualities through contemplation, one after another, then allow the mind to rest in its own natural state, they expand beyond any limitation, beyond any reference to self and other, to this individual or that. The immature aspects of these qualities— the melancholy weariness that contaminates compassion, the dull neutrality that substitutes for equanimity, the attachment that can taint love, the giddiness that can animate joy— are refined away. Compassion, equanimity, love, and joy fully ripen into the authentic, spontaneous, unobstructed qualities of buddha nature.

THE SIX PERFECTIONS: ENGAGING BODHICITTA

Bodhisattvas go beyond merely wishing for enlightenment; they engage in the path to enlightenment by practicing the six perfections (Skt. *paramitas*) of generosity, moral discipline, patience, joyful perseverance, concentration, and transcendent knowledge. For great bodhisattvas, perfect enactment of the path brings spontaneous, moment-to-moment opportunities to benefit beings combined with ongoing recognition of mind's absolute nature. For less mature practitioners, these six trainings refine away the self-centered perspective that obscures recognition of mind's nature and impedes fulfillment of the compassionate wish to lift others out of the pit of samsara. They also provide a measure of our progress in the sense that, in practicing discipline once, we accumulate the same merit as is gathered by practicing generosity twice, in practicing patience we accumulate twice the merit of discipline, and so forth, until we attain the boundless merit of transcendent knowledge.

Each perfection has three categories. Generosity (*jinpa*) is categorized as the offering of material objects, the offering of dharma, and the offering of protection. No material substance is too small to offer—even giving a morsel of food to a hungry dog or bird creates great merit if done with pure motivation and pure dedication. Presenting a precious object provides an opportunity to recognize the empty nature of the offering. Truly great bodhisattvas, by their realization of the emptiness of all things, are able to offer their own bodies selflessly. The Buddha, in a previous lifetime, gave his body to a famished tigress, and the Hinayana master Dharmarakshita cut the flesh of his thigh and offered it to a sick man who needed it for medicine. In that moment of pure altruism, the full potential to realize Mahayana awakened within him.

The offering of dharma is greater than the greatest gift of material wealth, yet we cannot fully pass on what we have not first fully learned and brought into meditative realization. Traditionally, the texts advise practitioners to remain in solitude and train their minds until they achieve stable meditation and the realization of emptiness. Chagdud Rinpoche's approach allows more leeway. Just as a five-year-old can hold the hand of and lend support to a toddler, so older students can help guide and inspire someone new to the dharma. Nevertheless, they must be skillful, not overestimating their maturity, underestimating their own need to develop, or exceeding their lama's authorization. The most certain means to offer the gift of dharma is by extending loving kindness to others and by providing an excellent example as a practitioner. And when our lama tells us to teach, we must do so tirelessly, unstintingly.

We also offer dharma by practicing on behalf of other beings, remembering them during formal meditation, or praying for them, or, if we have the capability, conducting ceremonies to meet their specific needs. Our ability to transform energies depends largely on our view and meditative concentration, as well as on the power of the lineage blessing and mantra. If we do not have full practice realization, however, we can enhance it through powerful motivation and dedication, and thereby create great benefit. Other infallible methods for reducing obstacles and obscurations include reading sutras, reciting prayers and confessions, making offerings, and saying mantras in the ears of animals. These practices, too, should be grounded in pure motivation and dedication.

Offering protection to those who are vulnerable and friendless, and particularly saving others' lives, represents the third mode of generosity.

Moral discipline (*tsult'hrim*) means refraining from bad

conduct, utilizing each opportunity to create merit, and working for the benefit of sentient beings. Bad conduct refers to the ten nonvirtues described in the chapter on karma; refraining from these requires a commitment to avoid doing the slightest harm to others and to watch the mind scrupulously, staring down even a subtle impulse toward nonvirtue before it translates into action of speech or body. If we find our motivation tainted with selfishness, our action will likewise be tainted. Vajrayana practitioners must be even more mindful, for they impair their vows even by viewing phenomena as ordinary rather than as a pure display of enlightened form, speech, and mind.

The second category of discipline, acquiring merit, refers to maintaining razor-sharp discrimination between what to accept and what to reject as appropriate actions of body, speech, and mind and conducting oneself accordingly. This creates a kind of economy that winnows out whatever is harmful or merely neutral and allows a natural, disciplined, moment-to-moment creation of merit through practice of the ten virtues, as described in the chapter on karma.

A third form of discipline manifests as work for the benefit of sentient beings. Each step of formal practice represents disciplined effort on behalf of others. Practice opens with the establishment of stainless bodhicitta motivation, is carried through as precisely as possible in order to fulfill this motivation, and concludes with pure dedication of the merit to the welfare of others. Outside of formal meditation, as we go about our daily business, we utilize the methods of dharma to maintain disciplined attentiveness in serving the needs of others. We might use our physical energy to help old or sick people or others in need, and our speech to soothe their fears and sorrows. Emptying our minds of preoccupation and distraction, we apply our powers of concentration to serving them. In this way, our efforts on behalf of others become a form of meditation.

Even an ordinary act like eating becomes extremely meaningful if we remember with compassion the animals that lost their lives to provide meat and the insects that lost their lives to provide vegetables, and if, through prayers and dedication, we honor the nourishment they provide. On an outer level food is offered to the Three Jewels, on an inner level to the mandala of deities who abide in our subtle channels and chakras. This offering becomes a source of merit that we dedicate to the beings whose very lives provided the food.

Finally, once our practice has brought us to a high degree of realization, we should enact the discipline of benefiting beings by attracting followers through our generosity, soothing speech, responsiveness to their needs, and demonstration of the sacred dharma.

Patience (*zodpa*), which Marpa the Translator declared the supreme virtue, is practiced through forbearance in the face of abusive treatment by others, endurance of hardship for the sake of dharma, and fortitude when hearing the teachings on emptiness. The recognition that negative conditions arise exactly according to one's karma—that in their very arising those karmic causes are being purified—adds a deeper dimension to patience. We could insist, quarrel, retaliate, or create more negativity, more cycles of suffering, but why do it? Why not instead patiently wait out the difficulty or even accelerate purification by cultivating loving kindness toward our antagonist? We see the negative karma and habits of this person coming to the fore. If we participate in his or her drama, we undermine our own progress in purification and our bodhicitta intention to benefit others. If anger escalates, our antagonist may face tortures in hell.

Since we would not choose this for anyone, even our worst enemy, we refrain from being the catalyst of that terrible fate by sustaining our own compassion and patience in the situation. If we have thoroughly realized impermanence, we can maintain patience with greater ease. We do not mire ourselves in difficulties; each challenge presents a valuable opportunity to practice dharma. Nor do we martyr ourselves. Knowing the power of patience, we realize that troubles eventually give way before the mind's ability to penetrate to the emptiness of events. What appears solid and real to one hemmed in by aversion seems fleeting and illusory to one steeped in patience. We see no need to flail at the turbulence of clouds.

During dharma practice, hardships manifest in many ways, from painful knees to major illnesses, from dire poverty to overwhelming worldly responsibilities, from hostile encounters to legions of friends who distract us from practice, from mind states that obscure the dharma with afflicted emotions to thought patterns that obscure it with words. The difficulties overcome by earlier great practitioners, beginning with the Buddha Shakyamuni, are legendary. Hardships that would have defeated anyone with lesser intention—exile, ridicule, assaults, demons, brutal climates, destruction of homelands and texts, physical separation from lamas—only strengthened practice. Patiently, great practitioners freed themselves from each strand of the binding web of illusion, from attachment and aversion and hope and fear, from all that stood between them and the revelation of absolute nature. When we meet with hardship in practice, we should not waver. Rather, we should reestablish our pure motivation and patiently deal with difficulties using whatever skill we command. If we penetrate the core of difficulty we will find nothing, no inherent reality, only the dreamlike residue of relative experience. Once we see this, patience gives birth to confidence.

The third aspect of patience is fortitude in the face of teachings on emptiness—teachings that dissolve the constructs of ordinary perception, the fictitious props and patterns we have relied upon for countless lifetimes. For some dharma students, such teachings produce fear, a sense that the ego is losing its grip, that solidity is giving way, that one might reel through space. Rules followed by rote must yield to transcendent view. Until the teachings on emptiness are thoroughly understood, first intellectually and then through meditative experience, we must quell any antagonism toward them with patience.

Joyful perseverance *(tsondrü)* variously translates as "diligence," "strenuousness," and "enthusiasm." Its three aspects are armor-like perseverance, effort, and insatiableness. Patience consists of working through each difficulty as it arises, while perseverance means continuing until completion, no matter how many difficulties arise in succession. Motivation to seek the enlightenment of all beings invests the practitioner with an armor-like perseverance that deflects lesser concerns and overcomes worldly fascinations, pleasures, and laziness. We become a bodhisattva warrior, living each moment to its utmost benefit, undaunted by hardships or the magnitude of the commitment. Commitment can be measured in many ways—by the accomplishment of a certain body of practice, by the attainment of certain qualities of mind or signs of meditation, and by perseverance until enlightenment.

Perseverance as effort means exerting ourselves, taking obstacles as part of our path, persisting in generating virtue, merit, and benefit for beings. When we clearly make dharma practice our priority, we can utilize the hidden potential of every phenomenon—even great spiritual hardship—to create

81

virtue. Sometimes meditation makes things seem worse by throwing our faults into sharp relief. We thought we were okay, but now it does not seem so. In those moments of honest self-assessment, it is hard not to become discouraged. If we persevere, however, we will have occasion to look back and take satisfaction in the transformations we have wrought through our practice.

We also gain confidence as we become adept at applying the methods of dharma to difficulties as they arise. Then, having set the highest goal possible, enlightenment for all beings, we experience an underlying joyousness as we persevere in accomplishing it. Joyful perseverance transcends inertia, laziness, and feeling overwhelmed. Although Buddhist teachings instill a profound awareness of samsaric suffering, those exemplary practitioners who persevered on the path— Shakyamuni, Milarepa, Longchen Rabjam, Shabkar, and others—found joy and freedom inconceivable to ordinary people.

The third aspect of perseverance is insatiableness. The human realm falls within the larger category of the desire realm, and an unceasing succession of desires characterizes the human experience. From its first thrust from the womb until its last gasp for breath, the body makes its physical demands. Speech expresses desires, both directly and indirectly, and influences others through communication. Mind, in its dualistic mode, continually formulates desires in terms of the phenomena it perceives: desires to be fulfilled, desires that flicker out, desires that fan into full-blown obsessions. Then, when the body dies, the desires of our lifetime dissipate like dreams, leaving only naked consciousness and karma.

At the moment of death and in the bardos afterward, only the dharma will benefit us. The worldly desires we have renounced, the spiritual training we have achieved, the benefit we have accomplished for others will be the sole sources of happiness and good fortune in future rebirths. The strength of our aspiration for enlightenment supplies the impetus to continue on our path. Therefore, we should be content in worldly matters but insatiable about dharma. We must not settle into complacency at a low level of practice; we must persevere until enlightenment.

Concentration (*samtan*) means directing the mind again and again into meditation until it is totally immersed, totally absorbed in it. The three aspects of concentration are described as childish concentration, effective concentration, and the meritorious concentration of bodhisattvas.

Childish concentration occurs when we achieve absorption but then become attached to temporary states of bliss, clarity, or nonconceptual stability. These states, called *nyam* in Tibetan, are like smoke from fire, merely a sign and not very important in themselves. Strong attachment to bliss can lead to samsaric rebirth in the desire realm of the worldly gods. Attachment to clarity and the fascinating visionary and psychic abilities that arise from clarity can lead to rebirth in the form realm of the gods, whereas attachment to stable nonconceptuality can lead to rebirth in the formless realm. Just like the meditative states themselves, these realms offer pleasure, but not liberation from cyclic existence. When a *nyam* experience arises in meditation, recognize it as ephemeral and cut it, refreshing the mind with bodhicitta intention or allowing the experience to dissipate into its own empty nature.

Effective concentration comes about when attachment to various types of *nyam* vanishes and concentration becomes effortless, yet we still rely on an intellectual sense of emptiness to counteract any grasping at appearances. The meritorious concentration of bodhisattvas occurs when the recognition of the empty nature of appearances becomes the nondual experience of absolute nature.

All three aspects of concentration depend on excellent meditation posture, preferably the seven-point posture of Vairocana. Hold the back very straight, tuck in the chin slightly, allow the eyes to gaze downward, cross the legs in vajra posture (that is, with the top side of the right foot placed on the left thigh and the top side of the left foot placed on the right thigh), lock the arms straight as they rest on the upper thighs (the hands curl into loose fists with the thumb pressing the bottom of the ring finger). Hold the shoulder blades up like vultures' wings and roll the tongue back toward the roof of the mouth. If it is impossible to maintain this posture, at least keep the back very straight, which allows the "winds," or energies, of the subtle body to move without obstruction and the mind to settle.

Transcendent knowledge (*sheyrab*) is recognition of the empty nature of all phenomena, the pervasive, single taste of emptiness throughout samsara and nirvana. The lama introduces the idea of emptiness in teachings on view. The understanding we gain from these teachings is clarified and applied through contemplation, and is finally realized nondually in meditation. We cannot say of anything that it exists or does not exist, that it comes or goes, that it is born or that it ceases, that it is one or many—all phenomena transcend any extreme imposed by words and concepts. Things appear, yet have no inherent reality. Understanding this, realizing it nondually in meditation, we gain the transcendent knowledge of practitioners of the great middle way, who do not deviate into fictitious views of reality.

From the vantage point of transcendent knowledge, we may describe the appearances of our relative reality by ten similes—as a dream, an apparition, a bubble, a magic show,

an optical illusion, a phantom city, a mirage, a flicker, a reflection, an echo. The underlying nature of this ephemeral
display of phenomena is absolute buddha nature, charac-
terized by seven "vajra qualities" that indicate unchangeable
essence—invulnerability, indestructibility, authenticity, in-
corruptibility, stability, unobstructedness, and invincibility.
Whereas in relative truth nothing holds and remains the
same, even for a microsecond, in absolute truth nothing
changes, nothing moves from the single, all-pervasive nature
of emptiness. So the Buddha taught, "Form is emptiness;
emptiness is form." The display of form is inseparable from
its empty nature; from emptiness the ceaseless display arises
spontaneously. When we have attained transcendent knowledge, awareness of the inseparability of the two truths becomes our ongoing experience.

In the context of transcendent knowledge, we practice
the first five perfections as an expression of absolute bodhicitta, as ceaseless activity on behalf of sentient beings. Generosity, exalted through transcendent knowledge, no longer
fetters itself with fictitious materialism. Attachments fall away
in the face of the empty nature of things and we perceive
offering substances as limitless manifestations of emptiness.
Acts of offering are experienced as illusory gestures between
offerer and recipient, who remain beyond dualistic delinea-
tion of self and other. Transcendent generosity becomes as
boundless, as equally pervasive as the radiance of the sun.

Discipline, enhanced by transcendent knowledge, allows
us a natural responsiveness and precision of body, speech,
and mind. As we stabilize our recognition of the empty nature of appearances, attachments and aversions based on fictitious reality lose their hold and no longer lead us into
nonvirtue. As our sense of self opens to its own empty nature, we are released from self-clinging and self-interest and
are no longer hindered in taking clear, disciplined action on

behalf of others. Ultimately, liberated from dualistic perception of self, other, and interaction, transcendent discipline represents a spontaneous, perfect expression of emptiness. Discipline becomes consummate freedom of action.

Patience, within the nondual experience of emptiness, finds no inherent reality in enemies and hindrances, no self for adversity to subvert, no intrinsic validity in emotions such as fear and animosity. Transcendent patience becomes effortless, beyond any need for patience.

Perseverance instilled with transcendent knowledge brings the insight that obstacles are simply illusions—transparent, insubstantial—that no longer separate us from our goal. Unopposed by obstacles, the forward force of perseverance transforms into effortless expansion of a single point, the recognition of absolute nature. Within this recognition, pure dharma qualities naturally unfold, enriching each moment to fullness. The goal having been attained, transcendent perseverance expresses itself as the continuity of enlightened intention to benefit sentient beings.

Concentration practiced within the sphere of transcendent knowledge has the qualities of easy, unwavering, concept-free attention. Without veering into fixation on form or emptiness, transcendent concentration maintains itself as ongoing recognition of absolute nature.

For themselves, bodhisattvas' attainment of ongoing transcendent knowledge is enough. Nothing more need be done. For the sake of confused, unhappy sentient beings, however, they continue to engage in the first five perfections from the open perspective of transcendent knowledge. Transcendent generosity, discipline, patience, perseverance, and concentration thus serve as bodhisattvas' activities to benefit beings spontaneously, constantly, within the realization of emptiness.

PROSTRATIONS: A MEDITATION
ON REFUGE AND BODHICITTA

Prostrations, performed as the two lines of refuge and the two lines of bodhicitta are recited, have the power to purify the three doors of body, speech, and mind of karmic defilements and conflicted emotions, particularly pride. The Buddha Shakyamuni told his disciple Ananda that even a single prostration accrues almost inexhaustible benefit. We might imagine that the ground covered by our body as we prostrate represents a golden land and, within it, each particle of dust an entire universe. The generosity of offering a single prostration equals that of offering as many universes as these particles of dust.

We complete one hundred thousand full-length prostrations while executing each movement as impeccably as possible and chanting the prayers clearly. We arouse reverence for the visualized embodiments of refuge as well as compassion for multitudes of beings visualized as prostrating simultaneously. Anyone who makes this effort and completes a hundred thousand prostrations becomes a more worthy receptacle for the precious Vajrayana teachings.

When Chagdud Rinpoche visited Tibet in 1987, he met a nun in her eighties who had performed millions of prostrations. When she was sixteen, she had determined that prostrations were her main practice and she focused on them for the next seven decades. She still continued to prostrate each day and enjoyed quite good health, tranquillity, and blissfulness of mind. When another student of Rinpoche's, an American from California, completed five hundred thousand prostrations, spontaneous songs of realization surged into his mind, even though he had never written poetry previously.

Rinpoche had other, athletic students who practiced with great energy and enthusiasm at the outset, then collided with the reality that they were not undertaking merely a strenuous physical exercise—prostrations have the effect of extraordinary purification. Soon these students struggled with aching knees, frustration, reluctance to continue. Why incorporate such spiritual hardship into their lives? Yet spiritual hardship represents a tremendous improvement over the ceaseless suffering of samsara, particularly the illnesses we experience when karmic seeds of negative actions suddenly ripen.

Rinpoche advised such students to check their motivation; he told them not to think of "getting the hard part out of the way" and moving on to other practices. He encouraged them to accept the difficulties with a certain joyousness, knowing that the pain represents purification, and to compare their discomfort with the sorrow of those devoid of refuge, who have no comprehension of why they suffer and no method to free themselves.

Prostrations give us an opportunity to practice on behalf of others by visualizing that they likewise prostrate, find refuge, and purify negative karma. When we prostrate with this expansive motivation, the practice becomes full-fledged bodhicitta activity and generates enormous merit.

Prostrations in the *Dudjom Tersar Ngondro* are performed reverently to Guru Rinpoche. We English-speaking practitioners are fortunate to have inspiring translations of Guru Rinpoche's biographies written by his consort and chief disciple, Yeshe Tsogyal, and by others. His life fulfilled the twelve deeds by which a buddha miraculously reveals him- or herself, and he accomplished the extraordinary activities of a Vajrayana master. During his time on this earth Guru Rinpoche created a powerful, vital bond between him and his succession of lineage holders, between him and those who practice his teachings or who even say his mantra with faith. In this decadent age, a time that the Buddha Shakya- muni and others prophesied would be conflict-ridden and spiritually diminished, the Vajrayana teachings of Guru Rin- poche illuminate the minds of beings more brilliantly than ever, and his compassionate intervention remains swift and sure.

For some practitioners, prostrations represent the first disciplined attempt to develop a Vajrayana visualization. We should approach visualization first by studying the written description and the explanation of the symbolism of Guru Rinpoche's form and by looking at a photograph or painted image. Chagdud Rinpoche sometimes recommends that stu- dents concentrate on a pictorial image, then look away. The image will remain in the mind's eye, but will evolve into a three-dimensional, rainbow-light representation. Gradually we become so familiar with the image that the details do not fade even though the visualization expands and becomes more radiant. We can see it as long as we focus our mind on it.

The eyes stay open as we prostrate and, in general, as we meditate. The interdependence of ordinary light and the luminous appearance of the visualized deity brings forth qualities of natural awareness. By closing the eyes we shut out light as well as ordinary visual phenomena, and create imploded, surreal images. Ordinary appearances are not the enemy of meditative concentration. If we do not grasp at them, do not assign concepts and emotional values to them, appearances tend to move naturally to the periphery of our attention as our meditative focus intensifies. We can avert distractions either by gently allowing them to subside or by energetically cutting through them.

In the process of practice, a deeper, more extraordinary sense of Guru Rinpoche's visual presence unfolds, one in accord with recognition of the pure nature of our own mind as well as the pure nature of the outer environment. We need not strive for this; if we practice with bodhicitta motivation and strong faith in Guru Rinpoche, it arises naturally as a sign of accomplishment.

Prostrations provide an excellent arena for the trainings of the six perfections. Generosity is enacted by the offering of homage and effort, and is enhanced by the inclusion of all other beings in our practice. Performing each movement with precision, reciting each prayer clearly, and maintaining the visualization train us in discipline. Patience comes to the fore when we deal with knee and muscle aches, as well as with the sickness and irritations that sometimes surface during this purifying process. Every person who has ever started with the first prostration and continued through the hundred thousandth has at some point had his or her joyful perseverance tested. Concentration is tested, too, in terms of holding a visualization while performing strenuous activity and not allowing distraction.

Transcendent knowledge arises from recognizing the empty nature of the visualization and of ourselves as we perform prostrations. This recognition comes to the fore particularly during the completion stage of the practice, when Guru Rinpoche dissolves into light, this light dissolves into us, and we rest nondually in mind's empty nature.

The powerful purificatory effect of prostrations dissipates the five poisons and allows the five wisdoms to transform mind's perception. Ignorance gives way to the wisdom of dharmadhatu, to the unobstructed space of enlightened awareness, beyond any boundaries imposed by concepts of existence or nonexistence. Attachment gives way to discriminating awareness, nondual recognition that the display of myriad phenomena arises from basic emptiness. Discriminating awareness utterly dissolves attachment by undermining any sense of phenomena's inherent existence. Anger dissipates into mirror-like awareness. Like images arising in a mirror, phenomena arise in mind's pure awareness—they arise and disappear and abide nowhere. How can there be aversion to what has no solid basis, no permanence, no more reality than figments of a dream? Pride—with its mixture of attachment to self and alienation from others, its fictitious assessments of superiority and inferiority—falls away before the wisdom of equanimity. Nondual recognition of the single taste and equal purity of all phenomena comes forth instead. Jealousy is transformed into its pure aspect, all-accomplishing wisdom. In the vast expanse of nondual perception, no causes for jealousy and envy emerge. Everything is accomplished just as it should be, without regard for who accomplishes it.

Patrul Rinpoche chose to include prostrations in the practice of guru yoga, as part of the seven-branch offering of prostrations, offerings, confession, rejoicing in virtue, requesting the turning of the wheel of dharma, requesting that the awareness holders not go beyond samsara, and dedication. In this context, we perform prostrations with the understanding that the symbolic lama—Guru Rinpoche in the *Dudjom Tersar Ngondro*—and our own teacher represent a single, all-encompassing source of refuge and bodhicitta. The lama embodies the Three Jewels in that his or her body is the sangha, his or her speech the dharma, and his or her mind the Buddha. The lama embodies the Three Roots in that his or her body is the guru, speech the chosen deity (*yi-*

dam), and mind the dakini (*khadro*). As well, the lama's qualities embody the wealth deities, and the lama's activities the dharma protectors. The lama embodies the Three Kayas in that his or her body is the nirmanakaya, speech the sambhogakaya, and mind the dharmakaya.

Although every other aspect of prostrations may remain the same, by recognizing the inseparability of the symbolic lama and our own teacher—a realization of pure guru yoga—we enrich our practice immeasurably. As His Holiness Dilgo Khyentse Rinpoche taught, "A single prostration made to our guru is more powerful than one hundred thousand prostrations to the buddhas and bodhisattvas of the ten directions of space." Each prostration expresses reverence for our own lama as Guru Rinpoche's actual manifestation. In the completion stage, resting in nondual meditation gives rise to a sense of union beyond words or concept. In daily life, it becomes easier to perceive our lama as a manifestation of Guru Rinpoche, to respond more mindfully, to experience a continuous flow of compassion and blessing.

MEDITATION INSTRUCTIONS

Visualize Guru Rinpoche in the space in front of you, luminous, exuding youthful vitality. He has a white complexion tinged with a red radiance. His expression—a slight smile, the furl of his brow, wide-open eyes—conveys compassion, but with a sense of alertness, the union of all peaceful and wrathful qualities. He sits in vajra posture on a thousand-petaled, multicolored lotus upon which rest a sun disk and a moon disk—the lotus a symbol of the innate purity of samsara and nirvana; the sun disk, enlightened compassion; the moon disk, pristine awareness. His right hand holds a five-pronged vajra to his heart; his left holds a skullcup filled

Padmasambhava (Guru Rinpoche)

with elixir of deathless realization, a long-life vase floating atop it.

In the crook of his left elbow rests a *khatvanga* (trident), its three prongs symbolizing emptiness, clarity, and compassion, the inseparable nature of the three kayas. The shaft of the trident is ornamented at the top with a skull, then a decayed head and a freshly severed head, representing atemporal realization of the three kayas. Below the heads are a longevity vase, a pair of crossed vajras that symbolize mastery of the four activities (subduing, increasing, magnetizing, wrathful intervention), and a skull drum from which waft silk scarfs. The khatvanga indicates the fruition of the third, or wisdom (transcendent knowledge and pristine awareness), empowerment (discussed later in the chapter on guru yoga), and its secret symbolism expresses Guru Rinpoche's inseparable union with his wisdom consorts, Mandarava and Yeshe Tsogyal.

Guru Rinpoche's robes include a white inner garment, which represents the pure, unstained vajra; the blue long-sleeved robe of a Vajrayana practitioner; red monastic robes; and the outer brocade cloak of a sovereign. He is adorned with a resplendent breastplate and earrings, and wears the lotus hat that liberates on sight, which is emblazoned with a sun and moon expressing skillful means and pristine awareness. Its brim forms three points, symbolizing the three kayas, and has five colors, symbolizing the five kayas—dharmakaya, sambhogakaya, nirmanakaya, svabhavikakaya, and the unchanging vajrakaya. The hat's peak is ornamented by a half vajra, symbol of unwavering concentration, and, extending from this half vajra, a vulture feather, symbolizing the highest view.

Visualize your father standing on your right side, your mother on your left, enemies prostrating in front of you, and demons behind you. The ranks of all sentient beings surround you and simultaneously prostrate, their recitation reverberating like the buzzing of bees. To perform a prostration, stand up straight with feet together. Bring your hands together in the "lotus bud" mudra (the base of the palm and the fingertips together, and thumbs slightly tucked in) and place them on the crown of the head, then to the throat and heart. As you place your hands on your crown, you offer homage to Guru Rinpoche's enlightened body, purify defilements and obscurations incurred through the avenue of your body, and establish the potential to realize nirmanakaya. At your throat, you offer homage to his enlightened speech, purify defilements and obscurations incurred through your speech, and establish the potential to realize sambhogakaya. Bringing your hands to your heart, you offer homage to his enlightened mind, purify your mind's obscurations, and establish the potential to realize dharmakaya.

The actual prostration is performed by dropping the body forward and stretching it full length on the floor, the arms outstretched in front. As you touch the floor, the five poisons—ignorance, attachment, anger, pride, and jealousy—dissipate. Again, with hands in the lotus bud mudra, bend your arms back and touch your hands to the top of your head, a gesture that acknowledges the blessing flowing from Guru Rinpoche. Then stretch your arms out once more and push yourself up. As you stand, the clearing away of the five poisons allows the five wisdoms to arise. Bring your hands into the lotus bud mudra for the third time and touch your heart in a gesture of reverence. Then, with a smooth motion, bring your hands to your crown and perform the next prostration.

Hold a mala in your left hand to count. A full-sized mala of one hundred and eight or one hundred and eleven beads may be used. However, it is easier to count with a prostration mala made up of twenty-seven large-diameter beads (large-diameter beads so the hand does not cramp), moving a stone each time the mala is circled and moving a hundred marker on your counters when you have completed four malas, that is, one hundred and eight prostrations. It is important to count with a mala rather than mentally keep track so that the mind remains fully engaged in the visualization, in refuge, bodhicitta, and devotion to Guru Rinpoche.

After finishing the number of prostrations scheduled for the session, move into the completion stage, visualizing that all beings dissolve into light, which dissolves into Guru Rinpoche, then into you. Rest there, in uncontrived, non-conceptual meditation. When thoughts intervene, dedicate the merit of your prostrations according to the dedication prayer in the ngondro practice, adding any others you choose.

If you are continuing the ngondro session through mandala offerings, the completion stage dissolution is performed after the mandalas. Having finished prostrations, maintain the visualization of Guru Rinpoche in the space in front of you and simply sit down to begin mandalas. Whether after prostrations or after mandalas, leave time to close the meditation properly. You will deny yourself profound opportunities for realization if, upon completion of prostrations, you simply walk away from the mat without dissolution and dedication.

MANDALA OFFERINGS

The two accumulations, merit and pristine awareness (*yeshey*),* must be fully accomplished in order to reach enlightenment. In ngondro, mandala offerings represent a direct method to gather these accumulations. The formal practice involves placing heaps of grains and jewels on a mandala pan and reciting an offering prayer. At the same time we visualize the entire cosmos, extending limitlessly, with its full store of wealth, beauty, and pleasure. Guru Rinpoche, embodiment of all sources of refuge, receives our offering, which creates immeasurable merit. Resting nondually in recognition of emptiness as the actual nature of the offering brings forth pristine awareness.

Within this cosmos lies our world system composed of Mount Meru, four continents that surround Meru in the cardinal directions, eight subcontinents, the sun, and the moon. Each continent is flanked by two subcontinents, which re-

*Transcendent knowledge—*sheyrab*—and pristine awareness—*yeshey*—have the same root, *shey*, which refers to knowledge or awareness. As noted earlier in the description of the six perfections, *sheyrab* means understanding emptiness as the fundamental basis of samsara and nirvana and maintaining an ongoing experience of this understanding. The *ye* of *yeshey* means atemporal and pristine, referring to awareness that has always been the true nature of mind as experienced nondually, without observer or observed.

semble it in shape and characteristics but are half its size. The subcontinents of our own continent of Dzambuling are named Ngayab and Ngayab-Zhan. The offering of the "three-thousand-fold universe" (meaning one thousand to the power of 3) refers to the billion such world systems that are encompassed by the enlightened influence of a single buddha such as our own Shakyamuni. Since countless other buddhas also exert their spheres of enlightened intention in countless other universes, the total number of world systems exceeds ordinary limitations of comprehension.

Through expansive visualization, the three-thousand-fold universe with its billion world systems—including the wealth, virtue, positive qualities, and attainments we ourselves have amassed in the course of innumerable lifetimes—is presented to Guru Rinpoche as the outer offering. Our body itself forms the inner offering, with the skin as a golden land, the spine as Mount Meru, the four limbs as gatekeepers, the eyes as the sun and moon, the five aggregates and elements as the five *dhyani* buddhas and their consorts, the eight consciousnesses and the objects of consciousness as the eight bodhisattvas and their consorts, and so forth. The secret offering is mind's nature as intrinsic awareness (*rigpa*) inseparable from emptiness.

Holding nothing back, we offer until we no longer grasp at appearances. Full and expansive mandala offerings purify the fundamental downfall of sentient beings, which is attachment. When attachment is purified, we attain the vast perspective that recognizes and experiences the empty nature of all phenomena. Within this recognition the delineations of our ordinary perspective—of ourselves as the offerer, mandalas as the offering, and Guru Rinpoche as the recipient of the offering—simply fall away and the single, empty nature of offerer, offering, and recipient becomes apparent to us. It is this realization that brings about the accumulation of pristine awareness.

By establishing the bodhicitta aspiration that our mandala offerings purify the obscurations and increase the merit of all sentient beings, we enhance the accumulation of merit to an inconceivable scale. Having set this motivation, we apply the six perfections to each step of the practice. Offering the best substances on the best mandala pan we can afford expresses generosity. Cleaning the pan and offering in a correct manner involve discipline. Offering even though we are tired or have other obstacles of mind and body requires patience. Offering consistently develops joyful perseverance. Banishing distractions while offering focuses concentration. Offering with transcendent knowledge of the essential emptiness of the offering makes evident our mind's absolute nature as pristine awareness.

In daily life, the mentality of offering can enrich the most ordinary actions. Each meal is an opportunity to offer food and drink to the mandala of deities within our body. Any pleasurable experience—the beauty of nature, the glitter of a luxurious shop, the freshness of a child's response—can be offered to Guru Rinpoche. We do not have to own a jewel or flowers or silk to envision them as boundless offerings to the buddhas and bodhisattvas and to sentient beings everywhere. This mentality of limitless generosity antidotes envy and a sense of impoverishment, and instills contentment.

The merit of such an attitude brings forth wealth, first in terms of mental well-being and then in terms of actual material abundance, as naturally as fire generates warmth and radiance. We must take care, however, that we are not motivated merely by selfish desire for prosperity, because when we die, we will not be able to take one penny with us. Only merit generated with the underlying intention to benefit beings will stand us in good stead during the transitions of death, the bardo, and future rebirth.

MEDITATION INSTRUCTIONS

Before the session, gather the mandala pan, the offering substances, and the cloth on which the offering will be made. The best pan is made of gold or silver, followed by copper, metal alloy, wood, or stone. The pan should be thoroughly cleaned before it is used. The finest offering substances consist of precious gems, gold, and silver, but bits of polished stone and jewelry are also appropriate. These jewels and stones should be washed. The offering should also include grain—barley, washed and dyed red or saffron yellow, is nice because it will not crumble as rice does. The cloth should be beautiful, strong, and large enough to catch the overflow of the offerings as they cascade from the pan.

In the session, begin by visualizing Guru Rinpoche in the space in front of you, understanding that he encompasses all sources of refuge. Pick up the mandala pan with your left hand and recite the hundred-syllable mantra while rotating the most delicate part of your right wrist in a clockwise direction on the top of the pan. This symbolically cleans the pan and provides a foundation for the offering by purifying the sins and obscurations of all beings.

Scoop up jewels and grain with your right hand and let them spill over the top of your fist, through the loop formed by your index finger and thumb. The first mound is spilled into the center of the pan and symbolizes Mount Meru, which rises up out of oceans of scented water, like a pyramid made up of four enormous steps and a flat top. The east side of the mountain is composed of crystal, the south side of lapis lazuli, the west side of ruby, the north side of gold.

In seven concentric rings around Mount Meru stand seven chains of golden mountains; in the swirling waters between these rings extraordinary sea creatures called nagas guard wish-fulfilling gems and other treasures; in the outer oceans beyond the seventh ring lie the four continents.

Spill jewels into a mound on the perimeter of the pan at the point most distant from you (the twelve o'clock position). This symbolizes the eastern continent of Lü P'hag Po, the land of wish-fulfilling jewels, shaped like a half moon and having clear skies, a radiant reflection of the crystal face of Mount Meru.

Spill jewels into a mound on the right perimeter of the pan (the three o'clock position). This symbolizes our own southern continent of Dzambuling, the land of wish-fulfilling trees, shaped like a trapezoid and having blue skies, a radiant reflection of the lapis lazuli face of Mount Meru.

Spill jewels into a mound at the bottom perimeter of the pan (the six o'clock position). This symbolizes the western continent of Balang Kyod, the land of wish-fulfilling cows, circular and with rosy skies, a radiant reflection of the ruby face of Mount Meru.

Spill jewels into a mound at the left perimeter of the pan (the nine o'clock position). This represents the northern continent of Draminyan, the land of effortless crops, square and with golden skies, a radiant reflection of the gold face of Mount Meru.

Once more, spill jewels into a mound in the eastern direction (twelve o'clock). This represents the offering of the sun with all its warmth and life-sustaining radiance.

Spill jewels into a mound in the western direction (six o'clock). This represents the offering of the moon with its silver illumination.

Tip the top of the mandala pan so that the barley spills toward you, symbolic of flowing blessings. Then clean the pan with the tender part of the right wrist, and repeat the offering of the seven mounds. Clear the pan, and repeat the offering once more. Repeat the two-line mandala prayer with the offering of each mound.

Now place the pan on the cloth in front of you. With your right hand scoop up the offerings of grain and jewels and spill them into a single, all-inclusive mound in the center of the pan, reciting one two-line prayer with each outpouring. With the left hand, count the recitations of the prayer on your mala. When you have completed one hundred and eight or one hundred and eleven recitations (depending on the number of beads on your mala), the full seven-mound offering is again repeated three times.

Once the mandala offerings for this session of ngondro practice are complete, Guru Rinpoche dissolves into light, which dissolves into you. The mind rests in nonconceptual meditation. When thoughts arise, you either continue your practice with Vajrasattva meditation or dedicate the merit of your mandala offerings to all sentient beings, many of whom are so bereft of merit that they do not have the wherewithal to sustain their lives, much less the great fortune to meet and practice a spiritual path. Offer them the virtue of your offerings so that they find both temporary and ultimate happiness through the two accumulations of merit and pristine awareness.

VAJRASATTVA

The next section of the ngondro consists of the purification practice of Vajrasattva (Tib. Dorje Sempa). Vajrasattva represents the mind aspect of all the buddhas, and "buddha" refers to one completely free of faults, who has fully realized the pure qualities of absolute nature. In practice, purification and the attainment of pure qualities are interdependent, because as we eliminate the stains and obscurations of nonvirtue, qualities such as compassion, love, and omniscience are uncovered and made obvious.

For countless lifetimes we have established patterns based on nonrecognition of our buddha nature. In our ignorant holding to self and other, we have constantly responded with attachment and aversion to the fleeting appearances of relative reality. Our attachment and aversion cause all manner of nonvirtue through body, speech, and mind. These can be generally categorized as the ten nonvirtues described in the chapter on karma, but negative actions are endless in their variety and provide countless karmic causes for suffering.

All beings find themselves in predicaments arising from their self-created negative karma. The bodhisattva Vajrasattva, before crossing the threshold of enlightenment, surveyed the realms of sentient beings. Compassion arose in his

103

mind as he saw how most were mired in their own nonvirtue and perceived no way out. He then made a bodhisattva vow: "May all sentient beings, by merely hearing, remembering, or uttering my name in prayer, be purified of their karmic negativity and be liberated from the depths of cyclic existence." Thus, Vajrasattva is aware of whatever nonvirtue takes place and can manifest as a force of purification for the benefit of beings.

We use the "four powers" as steps toward full purification. The first power consists of invoking a wisdom being as witness—in ngondro, we specifically visualize Vajrasattva in union with his consort, Dorje Nyema. The second power is that of acknowledging where we have gone astray and the harm we have caused, as well as feeling genuine remorse for what we have done. Most of us cannot remember all our downfalls in this life, much less in countless past lives. If, however, we thoroughly check our minds when some negativity becomes obvious, we will probably see the tendency that led to it and can surmise what kind of harm it caused in the past. An honest, careful person will not remain blind to his or her faults or to their source and their ramifications. All aspects are confessed with regret to Vajrasattva.

The third power of purification consists of a vow not to repeat a particular mistake. Without this commitment it is very difficult to extricate oneself from the cycles of nonvirtue, the cycles of rebirth. This vow concentrates tremendous power of purification. For example, in India, where one's occupation used to be completely determined by caste, there once lived a butcher. He hated his work, saw the suffering it caused the animals, wished to work at something else, but could not. He was inescapably of the butcher caste, as had been his father and his grandfather and his forefathers for generations. He mulled over what to do and at last concluded that although he must remain a butcher in the daytime, at night he would keep a vow never to kill or harm anything. For the rest of his life he kept this vow, and he lived on for many years.

A contemporary of this butcher was an arhat who had the power to visit all realms. One night, sometime after the butcher's death, the arhat was on one of his extraordinary journeys when he came across a celestial mansion in which a worldly god was sitting on a throne, being served nectar and delectable foods by four beautiful offering goddesses. As the arhat marveled at the amazing good karma that had generated such bliss, the sun rose and the scene transformed. The celestial mansion became a molten iron box, the four beautiful goddesses became four minions of hell, who brutally beat their captive and forced fiery lava down his throat, and the bliss became unimaginable torment. When the arhat inquired, he learned that the god/captive was a butcher who had killed by day but had kept a vow not to kill or harm by night.

The fourth power of purification occurs when the deity's nectar or light saturates us and cleanses all stains and defilements. At first it may not be easy to experience this blessing because of our strong habit of holding the body as solid and impervious. However, as our meditation deepens and we gain transcendent knowledge of our own nature as emptiness, we can feel nectar flowing from Vajrasattva into us as though our body were a mere sheath of consciousness.

Through Vajrasattva we can purify the whole mass of our defiled samaya commitments, including broken refuge vows, downfalls in our bodhisattva training, and impairments of our Vajrayana view. It is extremely important that Vajrayana practitioners do Vajrasattva purification every day, because their vows are so difficult to maintain. As soon as the mind slips from the view of the inherent purity of all appearance—as soon as we judge those feces as dirty, that person as stupid or irritating, that sickness or feeling as bad—we have defiled our Vajrayana vow to adhere to the recognition of the innate purity of all phenomena. Grosser infractions are to drop practice commitments, to fall into conflict with sangha members, or to displease our lama.

In his infinite mercy, Vajrasattva has provided us with a method to remedy all broken vows. If we allow defilements to accumulate, this will affect our practice. Our mind may become dull and unreceptive, we may become sluggish or sick, few positive signs will arise to encourage us, and we may lose confidence, despairing of ever reaching enlightenment. Even if this has already begun to occur, we can use the four powers of purification to stop the erosion of our spirituality and regain the clarity and momentum of our path.

Vajrasattva represents a superb practice to bring into daily life. We can silently chant the mantra and visualize Vajrasattva and consort over our head and over the heads of others, white nectar flowing into all of our crown chakras. If we maintain the practice as we go about our ordinary activities, we will become sensitive to any negative impulse that arises in our mind. It is easy to refine negativity away at that point, before it flares into a full-fledged emotion or obsession, before it carries over into nonvirtuous actions of body or speech.

We shouldn't be discouraged, however, if our nonvirtuous tendencies and negative karma seem denser and more intractable than before we began Vajrasattva practice. As we focus attention on patterns ingrained over many lifetimes of obliviousness, seeing them brings undeniable pain. Yet, equally, we can rejoice that we have discovered an unsurpassed method of purification that can lift any practitioner from the very depths of samsara.

Vajrasattva with Consort

MEDITATION INSTRUCTIONS

Rest the mind, dropping thoughts about past, present, future. The mind's natural emptiness spontaneously gives rise to a brilliantly white, thousand-petaled lotus in full bloom with a moon disk in its center, a forearm above your crown chakra. Atop the moon disk sits your root lama in the luminous white form of Lama Vajrasattva in union with his consort, Dorje Nyema, symbolizing the union of appearance and emptiness. He embraces her, holding a vajra—an emblem of the qualities of absolute nature—in his right hand at the center of her back. In his left hand, which rests on his thigh, he holds a bell, symbol of transcendent knowledge. His legs are in vajra posture; Dorje Nyema's legs are clasped around his waist. In her left hand she holds a skullcup filled with blood, symbolizing transcendence of samsaric attachment. In her right hand she holds a curved knife (*drigug*), which symbolizes self-clinging cut by selflessness.

The pair are adorned with the five silken garments of the sambhogakaya deities: a scarf skimming the shoulders and encircling the arms, a headdress made of five-colored pendants, a bolero, a belt, and pantaloons for Vajrasattva and a short skirt for Dorje Nyema. They are also ornamented with the eight jewels of the peaceful sambhogakaya deities: a crown; earrings; short, midlength, and long necklaces; bracelets, armlets, and anklets.

Their forms express the nine signs of wisdom bodies: pliancy as a sign that ignorance has been purified; perfect proportions as a sign that anger has been purified; well-toned musculature as a sign that desire has been purified; delicacy as a sign that pride has been purified; youthfulness as a sign that jealousy has been purified; clearness as a sign that stains have been purified; radiance as a sign of all excellent qualities; attractiveness as a sign of the perfection of the thirty-two noble marks and eighty excellent signs; splendor and blessing as a sign of having vanquished all obscurations and obstacles.

Holding the visualization of Vajrasattva and Dorje Nyema, focus on Vajrasattva's heart, where there is a white, eight-petaled lotus with a moon disk in its center and, above the moon disk, a crystal vajra with a sun disk in the sphere that separates the pronged ends of the vajra. Above this sun disk hovers the white seed syllable *Hung*. The disk's perimeter is marked with the six-syllable mantra *Om Vajrasattva Hung,* which faces outward. *Om* is at the top of the perimeter, toward Vajrasattva's front; the other mantra syllables are spaced evenly around the perimeter. When mantra repetition begins, they generate an intense radiance that coalesces as nectar and fills the deities' forms.

The nectar then drips down through the point of union of Vajrasattva and his consort into your crown chakra. Gradually it fills your entire body with milky radiance and bliss. Simultaneously all of your impurities are forced out through the body's orifices and the skin's pores. Sins and defilements emerge as slimy black, polluted water; sickness as blood and pus; demonic entities as vermin, insects, and spiders.

Waiting in a huge crevasse nine layers below in the earth are all your karmic creditors, those whose debt you have incurred through the harm you have caused them. As foulness falls on them, they receive it as an offering of what most satisfies them, as the source of limitless, inexhaustible bliss. Your karmic debts are completely repaid.

At the close of the session Vajrasattva and consort dissolve into light, which dissolves into you. Rest inseparably with the mind of Vajrasattva, the absolute purity that is the nature of your own mind.

GURU YOGA

It is imperative to exert yourselves in the practice of guru yoga until you have grasped the vital essence of this practice. If you do not do this, your meditation will grow weaker and even though it creates some benefit, many obstacles will arise. Producing genuine understanding in the mind is not easy, so pray to your guru with uncontrived, fervent devotion. Eventually you will receive direct transmission from the enlightened mind of the guru and extraordinary realization, beyond expression in words, will arise.

His Holiness Dudjom Jigdral Yeshe Dorje

The guru is like a wish-fulfilling jewel granting all the qualities of realization . . . he is the equal of all the buddhas. To make any connection with him, whether through seeing him, hearing his voice, remembering him, or being touched by his hand, will lead us toward liberation. To have full confidence in him is the sure way to progress toward enlightenment.

His Holiness Dilgo Khyentse Rinpoche

No one ever reached enlightenment without a mastery of guru yoga so profound that he or she was able to receive—without any resistance, distortion, or doubt—the transmission of the guru's pristine awareness. The Buddha Shakya-

110

muni himself said that, without the lama, there can be no buddha. The supreme good fortune to receive this mind-to-mind transference of realization arises from pure samaya with our lama and preparation of our mind through purification and the accumulation of vast stores of merit. Our mind stands ready and receptive, like a well-tilled field waiting to be sown.

Transmission may occur in a formal empowerment or teaching, or it may come when we are least expecting it. Stories abound of Buddhist practitioners experiencing dramatic, nondual revelations of absolute nature when their teacher struck them. The most famous of these stories concerns the mahasiddha Tilopa striking Naropa, who had begun as a great Buddhist scholar, then completely surrendered to Tilopa's instructions even when they seemed exceedingly eccentric. After his years of devoted service to his guru, Naropa's moment of supreme realization dawned when Tilopa suddenly hit him on the head with a shoe. From that point on, his realization matched Tilopa's—there was no longer any separation between his mind and his teacher's.

More recently, in the first decades of this century, the previous incarnation of His Holiness Penor Rinpoche was entrusted into the care of the unsurpassed master Khanpo Ngaga. Because he was an undisputed incarnation (*tulku*) of Drubwang Pema Norbu, everyone knew the boy had elements of greatness, yet he seemed a bit dense for one who had embodied brilliant qualities of scholarship and meditative realization in his past lifetimes.

One day Khanpo Ngaga and the young tulku went for a walk. When they arrived at the top of a hill outside the monastery, the boy respectfully laid out his *zan* (a Buddhist robe, resembling a shawl) on the ground as a seat for his lama. Khanpo Ngaga sat down and handed the tulku his shoes, an unusually fine pair that someone had brought from China and offered to him. As the boy placed the shoes on the hillside, one of them tumbled down and fell into a mud puddle. With lightning swiftness, Khanpo Ngaga snatched the other shoe and whacked the tulku's head with it. For some moments the boy stood dazed, but far from knocking him stupid, the jolt opened wondrous recognition of the empty nature of things. In the days that followed, from that single glimpse of absolute truth arose vast understanding. No scholarly discourse, however arcane, remained beyond the tulku's comprehension. From that point onward, the dharma qualities he had cultivated in his past lifetimes blossomed naturally.

Usually, however, transmission unfolds gradually rather than in a single, dramatic moment. Each time we hear the teachings, their meaning for us reaches a deeper level. Each time we interact with our lama, our resistance softens. We begin to see the barriers set up by our own karmic patterns and habitual concepts. The teachings of the dharma provide us with manifold methods to overcome those barriers, and each time we use them successfully we increase both our faith in the effectiveness of dharma and our faith in the lama's realization. Our inner resonance with the lama grows stronger, and our longing for union, our devotion, our reliance on the lama evolve into a kind of spontaneous responsiveness.

Outwardly everything may appear the same; inwardly our heart is full and our mind expansive. Boundaries fall away before transcendent knowledge of the empty nature of everything. We realize that all along the lama's realization has penetrated the dense layers of our obscurations. Now, as those layers clear away, our openness allows us to receive our teacher's mind-to-mind transmission, nondually, beyond words. Words cannot capture the experience or even the individual qualities of the lama's pristine awareness—boundless compassion, transcendent knowledge, nondual recognition of the three kayas as inseparable. Naming points the way, but in actual moments of transmission, all the complexities of names and concepts fall away before infinite, ineffable simplicity. We rest in the absolute lama. Anyone who has truly experienced this extraordinary transmission has no less than the deepest reverence for his or her guru and will never turn back before attaining enlightenment.

We begin guru yoga in the *Dudjom Tersar Ngondro* by visualizing ourselves as Vajrayogini and, in the space in front of us, Guru Rinpoche, inseparable from our own lama, embodiment of the quintessential form of all lineage lamas. In the context of the practice, Guru Rinpoche reigns as the symbolic lama, the focus of our prayers and aspirations, the source of blessings and empowerments. We pray to Guru Rinpoche, imploring him to hold us in continuous compassion, during this and future lifetimes and in the intermediate states between lifetimes.

Having prayed in this manner, we begin repetition of the Vajra Guru mantra—*Om Ah Hung Vajra Guru Padma Siddhi Hung*—a mantra so powerful it brings liberation to whoever continually recites it with devotion. In the course of ngondro, we recite one million two hundred thousand mantras, one hundred thousand for each of the twelve syllables. We should open to the direct perception that repeating the Vajra Guru mantra actually manifests Guru Rinpoche's presence, that its resonance represents him in the form of sound, that the mantra as speech remains inseparable from his body and mind.

The Vajra Guru mantra incorporates the essence mantras of all enlightened ones. *Om* invokes the blessing of Guru Rinpoche's enlightened body, vajra body; *Ah* invokes his vajra speech; *Hung,* his vajra mind. *Om Ah Hung* together indicates that Guru Rinpoche encompasses the inseparable three kayas.

The mantra also holds the power of the five aspects of pristine awareness, usually referred to as the "five wisdoms." *Vajra* purifies anger and invokes the mirror-like wisdom of the vajra family. *Guru* purifies pride and invokes the wisdom of equanimity of the ratna family. *Padma* purifies attachment and invokes the discriminating wisdom of the padma family. *Siddhi* purifies jealousy and invokes the all-accomplishing wisdom of the karma family. *Hung* purifies ignorance and invokes the wisdom of dharmadhatu of the buddha family.

Vajra Guru (*dorje lama*) taken together indicates the unsurpassed realization and qualities of Guru Rinpoche as a supremely accomplished being who has brought the path of Vajrayana to consummation. *Vajra* means that, diamond-like, his recognition of absolute nature cuts through ordinary concepts and poisonous emotions. He has attained the supreme mastery of the inseparable three kayas and accomplished all qualities of enlightenment through transcendent knowledge and pristine awareness. *Guru* means that Guru Rinpoche embodies the gathered qualities of all enlightened buddhas of past, present, and future.

Padma indicates that Guru Rinpoche is the nirmanakaya emanation of Buddha Amitabha, lord of the lotus family. *Siddhi* refers to the two kinds of accomplishment, ordinary siddhis such as supernormal powers and the supreme siddhi of enlightenment. *Hung* invokes Guru Rinpoche's blessing to grant the two siddhis.

The mantra recitation concludes with the bestowal of the four empowerments (see the meditation instructions below).

The realization of this formal practice extends into daily life, where it forms the basis of pure perception. All form is experienced as the form of the lama, all sound as the speech of the lama, all mental events as the mind of the lama. This sacred outlook imbues every moment with the potential of guru yoga.

Guru Yoga

MEDITATION INSTRUCTIONS

Attachment to ordinary appearances and corporeality subside. You instantaneously transform into the female deity Vajra Yogini (Dorje Naljorma), luminous, beautiful, sixteen years old, naked except for a garland of flowers and five bone ornaments that symbolize the first five perfections. Vajra Yogini herself represents the sixth perfection of transcendent knowledge. She has a peaceful face and white skin that glows with a red radiance. She stands on a lotus, moon disk, and corpse—the lotus expressing the pure nature of emptiness, the moon a symbol of compassion, and the corpse the conquest of ego. Her right knee is slightly bent and her right foot flexed back a bit. In her right hand she brandishes a knife with a short, vajra-capped handle and a curved blade that is turned inward, symbolizing the cutting of self-clinging by selflessness. She holds in her left hand at her waist a skull-cup of blood, symbolizing transcendence of samsaric attachment. Her three eyes gaze longingly into space. Guru Rinpoche manifests before her in the form visualized for prostrations and mandala offerings.

Yearningly, with devotion, pray for Guru Rinpoche's compassion and blessing. As you recite the Vajra Guru mantra one hundred and eight times or in multiples of that number, receive purification and blessing in the form of light.

At the conclusion of mantra recitation, receive the four empowerments from Guru Rinpoche, as follows. Visualize brilliant white light radiating from an *Om* on Guru Rinpoche's forehead to your own forehead, purifying your defiled actions of body. The light confers the "vase empowerment," which authorizes you to practice the visualizations and sadhanas (liturgies) of the development stage and establishes the potential to attain enlightened body and nirmanakaya realization.

Yeshe Tsogyal

Ruby red light radiates from a red *Ah* in Guru Rinpoche's throat to yours, purifying defiled speech. The light confers the "secret empowerment," which authorizes you to recite the mantra and to practice the yoga of channels and winds and establishes the potential to attain enlightened speech and sambhogakaya realization.

Sapphire-blue light radiates from a *Hung* in Guru Rinpoche's heart to yours, purifying mental defilements. The light confers the "wisdom" (transcendent knowledge and pristine awareness) empowerment, which authorizes you to practice the effortful completion stage, as well as the yogas of inner heat and great bliss, and establishes the potential to attain enlightened mind and dharmakaya realization.

Finally, from Guru Rinpoche's forehead, throat, and heart, lights simultaneously radiate forth to your heart, purifying intellectual obscurations and obscurations caused by habit. This intense surge of the three lights confers the "word empowerment," which authorizes you to practice the effortless completion stage and establishes the potential to realize svabhavikakaya, that is, the single nature of the three kayas. In an alternative visualization orange light radiates from a *Hri* in Guru Rinpoche's navel to your navel and bestows this fourth level of empowerment.

These empowerments are acknowledged by a line of recitation, then sealed with the mantra *Vajra Guru Kaya Waka Tsitta Siddhi Hung.*

Finally, recite the last two lines of the guru yoga section. The visualization dissolves into light, which dissolves into you. Rest the mind inseparably in Guru Rinpoche, in the experience of awareness and emptiness inseparable (*rigtong*), in the nature of the absolute lama.

TRANSFERENCE OF CONSCIOUSNESS

The *Dudjom Tersar Ngondro* includes a very abbreviated form of *p'howa*, transference of consciousness into the pureland. By visualizing the Buddha Amitabha above our head, we train ourselves to direct our consciousness toward Dewachhan, his pureland of great bliss, when we die. Even if we are not able to fully accomplish this level of transference at the moment of death—perhaps because we die suddenly amid great chaos—this training equips us with the means to find liberation in the bardos after death, or at least an auspicious rebirth. This is assured for two reasons.

First, exiting of the consciousness from the crown chakra leads to a higher rebirth than does its exiting from one of the lower orifices. Second, Amitabha's enlightened intention establishes that all those who pray to him with faith and who longingly direct their mind toward him will find rebirth in his pureland. At the moment of death, the consciousness can move upward along the avenue we have prepared by visualizing Amitabha over our head. This provides a shortcut out of samsaric suffering. Having attained the pureland, we can remain until enlightenment, receiving the dharma transmissions that finally clear residual obscurations, or we can choose to come back and continue our spiritual development in this realm. In either case we gain great ability to benefit beings.

This p'howa training, like the practices that precede it in the ngondro, can be undertaken as an aspect of guru yoga if we understand that our lama is inseparable from Amitabha. We need take only a small step beyond the recognition of the lama as inseparable from Guru Rinpoche, because Guru Rinpoche is the nirmanakaya emanation of Amitabha. Another way to fathom the meaning of our lama's inseparability from Amitabha is to ask, "Who will I rely on when I die? Who really has the power to support me in that moment?" Most of us would turn to our lama, knowing that his or her power and blessing surpass any ordinary kindness or help a doctor or a loved one could offer us. Our lama's ability to extend help in life-threatening situations and the transitions of death, the bardo of becoming, and rebirth stems from his or her realization of buddha nature, no different from Guru Rinpoche's or Amitabha's. This power supports us even when the lama is not directly present.

Some years ago, a Western practitioner was traveling by bus in the mountains of northern India. As the vehicle pulled to a stop, it lost its brakes, swerved to avoid an oncoming bus, and toppled down a steep mountainside, rolling over and over, crushing passengers, until it crashed into a ravine hundreds of feet below, a crumpled heap of twisted metal and broken bodies. Thrown out the back door in the first moments of this nightmarish sequence, the student saw, in a kind of freeze-frame, the bus hover in space, about to slam into her. Suddenly everything changed and her lama, Thinley Norbu Rinpoche, appeared, seemingly a thousand feet tall, riveting her attention. Mentally, she implored, "What do I do?" Instantly she knew his answer and began calling out the Vajra Guru mantra at the top of her lungs.

The bus somehow missed her and, though terribly injured, she survived. Sixty others died that day.

In the mid-1980s, while Chagdud Rinpoche still lived in Oregon, he and his students were meditating in the center's shrine room one night when Rinpoche abruptly interrupted the practice. "Pray strongly now," he urged, "or maybe something terrible will happen." The next day we learned that a close student of his, driving down the interstate, had fallen asleep at the wheel and spun off the highway. Fortunately, she was unharmed.

More recently, a child in Chagdud Rinpoche's sangha died in California after a long illness. Rinpoche was in Moscow, but he immediately received a call requesting him to perform p'howa. Sangha members were simultaneously practicing p'howa in the deceased child's room. After some time Rinpoche telephoned and instructed the sangha members to check for the physical signs of accomplishment. They did, but reported that none had yet appeared. Rinpoche exclaimed, "I am sure of the signs. Look again!" This time he explained carefully how to check, and when the students looked again, the signs were clearly evident.

Distance, even death, does not separate us from our lama. Only our own wavering faith and obscurations come between us. If by prayer and meditation in this lifetime we can overcome these obstacles, in death we can find ultimate unity with the absolute lama.

MEDITATION INSTRUCTIONS

Visualize Buddha Amitabha, inseparable from your own lama, sitting in vajra posture on a thousand-petaled multicolored lotus, sun disk, and moon disk that hover a forearm's distance above your crown chakra. As lord of the lotus fam-

Buddha Amitabha

ily, he radiates brilliant ruby-red light, a sign of his limitless love and compassion for sentient beings, as well as his ability to magnetize and bring forth their pure awareness. He wears the nirmanakaya robes of a monk, and his hands rest in the gesture of meditative equipoise, holding a sapphire begging bowl filled with the nectar of immortality. Meditate until you feel unswerving confidence in his presence and deep longing for union with his enlightened mind. At that point recite the prayer for the blessing to accomplish the profound path of p'howa. Then dissolve the visualization and allow your mind to rest in uncontrived meditation.

DEDICATION OF MERIT

The dedication prayer begins with a distillation of *chod*, a practice of cutting self-clinging and offering with consummate generosity: "Now my body, possessions and the root of my virtue all together I give without clinging to all beings, who have been my parents." By transcendent knowledge of the empty nature of all things, we are able to offer everything, even our own body, without any attachment whatsoever. We first offer to the glorious Three Jewels and Three Roots and to the guests of honor, including the dharma protectors and wealth deities. It is our hope that they will find our offering completely delightful, that our merit will increase and, with it, our ability to carry out their activities to benefit sentient beings. We then offer to the lower guests, the guests of compassion, meaning sentient beings, and our karmic creditors whom we have wronged previously. By the blessing of wisdom beings, the merit of our generosity, and the power of our prayer, our offering is transformed into whatever satisfies the lower guests—into medicine for the sick, wealth for the poor, food for the famished, and so on.

With the final line of the ngondro practice, "May great benefit be accomplished without obstacle for all beings," we dedicate the virtue of the practice itself. When we conclude a practice session and pause on the cusp of meditation and postmeditation, we have come to a pivotal point. We can stand up, walk away, and feel full and satisfied with our accomplishment. Or we can offer that accomplishment to the welfare of all, adding the virtue we have created through practice to the store of merit of sentient beings. If we conclude without dedicating the merit, we risk everything—merit can be destroyed by anger, saturated with pride, diminished through jealousy. If we offer our merit through dedication, we only increase it. Like water added to the ocean, nothing limits its expansion. Like oil added to a lamp, it increases the illumination of everything within the sphere of its radiance.

Let us imagine two bodhisattvas standing on the threshold of enlightenment. For countless lifetimes they have served sentient beings selflessly. Their realization is equal, for enlightenment is absolute. Still, at that moment, their dedication has unsurpassed relevance, for it will determine the reach of their enlightened intention, whether their benefit will be direct, like Vajrasattva's or Amitabha's, or whether it will be less accessible. For this reason, even now, when enlightenment seems far in the future, we should begin perfecting our prayers of dedication. However exalted our aspirations, may they find their highest fulfillment!